MW00897438

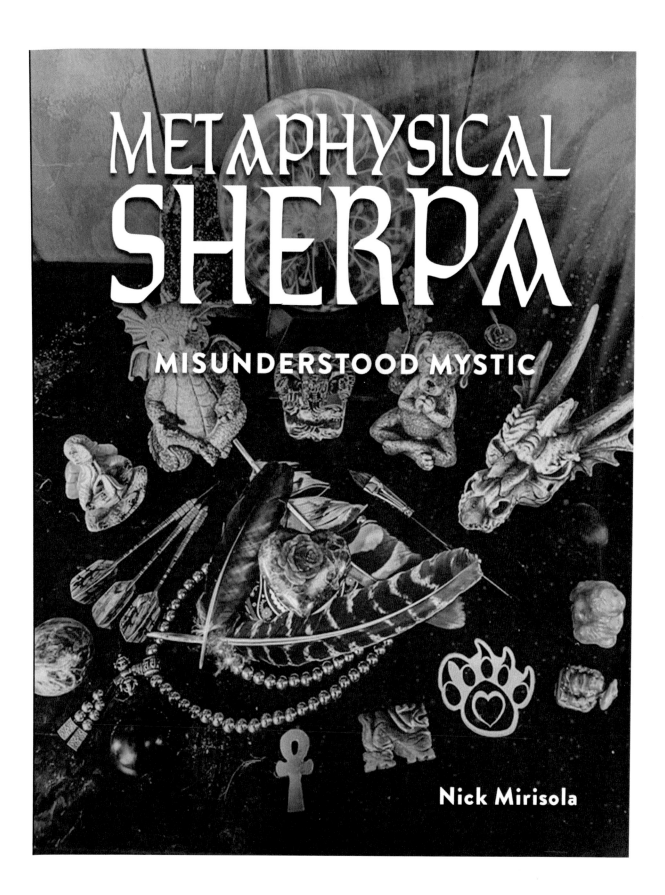

METAPHYSICAL SHERPA

MISUNDERSTOOD MYSTIC

Nick Mirisola

Metaphysical Sherpa:

Misunderstood Mystic

Nick Mirisola

Table of Contents

11

Preface

I would like to introduce my book with a review written by my Zen Master Meditation Practitioner Certification teacher:

"Nick Mirisola offers a birds eye view of his intriguing journey of exploration of self, testing the limits, clashes with police, sleep deprivation, and experiences that ultimately lead to his awakening. What is most beautiful is his unapologetic truth in his ever manifesting life, passing through its constraints, while pursuing a way to experience joy, music and healing on his own terms. What makes life so majestic is our ability to live it from our own unique perspective, and in this book, Nick shares that tale with us!"

~ Sufani Weisman-Garza,

Author of The Sculptured Soul

& True Stories Of An Urban Shaman

Synopsis

The Elevator Pitch

The name I go by is Nick, but my full name is Nicholas David Mirisola. Some of my friends call me "Zen," and my license plate says DUDDHA. I was born a western horoscopic Sagittarius sun and moon sign, Libra rising, on Thanksgiving Day in 1981, during the Chinese zodiac year of the golden rooster. So a wise-ass Cock-A-Doodle-Doo to you, and thank you for everything, everyone!! It could be worth noting that by the 13 zodiac sign Sidereal system that has been updated to reflect the changed positions of the stars since the creation of the 12 sign system of Greek origin, I am a Scorpio sun and moon sign, with Sagittarius in my south node, which is the area that defines what I am over-equipped within my birth chart. The name Nicholas means victory of the people, David means friend or beloved, and Mirisola means reflection of the Sun.

At a time when the Mayan calendar, the Native American prophecies, astrologers, and the 'New Age Movement' predicted the end of one cycle of time, age and era, and the dawn of a new one, I associated intensely with the spiritual, psychic, and 'New Age' phenomenon known as The Indigo Children. Indigo children were a cross-cultural phenomenon where clairvoyants noticed a wave of children born with indigo auras who were fiercely independent, interconnected, intuitive, and deeply spiritual souls. They are trailblazing society in a global effort toward progress, raising consciousness and vibrations, soulful living, and a renewed sense of spiritual community. Indigo is the color of the third eye chakra and is associated with the pineal gland in the brain, or third eye, which has light-sensitive cells in it like the ones in the two ocular eyes.

It is also associated with the seat of the soul and the mind's eye to the Egyptians. Indigo children have frequently been misunderstood, mislabeled, misdiagnosed, and misinterpreted. Many were prescribed stimulants for a misdiagnosis of attention deficit disorder when, in reality, they were abstract and deep critical thinkers, uninterested in much of the tedious, trivial monotony of the public school systems, and outside the box in their approach and priorities in comparison with the rather lackluster and corrupted norms of society.

I experienced a misdiagnosis of ADD around the age of 18. It was one of my first introductions to the deeply flawed mental health system, which, over the following two decades or so, repeatedly misunderstood, misdiagnosed, misinterpreted, and mislabeled me, much to my detriment, in addition to putting my friends and family through many unwanted stresses and issues to deal with. From bipolar disorder to schizoaffective disorder, I have been Guinea pigged against my will for nearly two decades on every family of drugs for the diagnoses mentioned above until I eventually ran out of unsuccessful, side-effect-ridden chemicals to try.

It was at that point that my psychiatrist and guardian decided that I had to choose at least one pop psychiatry anti-psychotic drug because they were obsessed with medicating me the big pharma way, which, by the way, is known as a chemical lobotomy in natural medicine disciplines, and casually referred to by patients and staff as "The Thorazine Shuffle." The drug I settled on for the last decade was a contraindicated dopamine inhibitor with an unknown clinical mechanism known as Prolixin, originally a brand name. Keep in mind that dopamine is considered a happiness, motivation, reward, and emotional "feel good" chemical, and I have recently found out that I have a genetic predisposition for higher than average dopamine levels in my prefrontal cortex, the highest evolved area of the brain, in addition to a sensitivity to emotional stress in my genes too.

It should also be noted that Buddhist meditators have shown above-average dopamine levels in studies, too. After over a decade of being forced to take it against my will, I only recently discovered that Prolixin is contraindicated in cases of depression, which plagued me since my childhood, and it is also contraindicated for people who use hypnotics, which the medical marijuana I use as an antidepressant and anti-anxiety drug is classified as. It is also contraindicated in cases of suspected brain damage.

The doctors' inhibition of my dopamine results in a state of mind which is analogous to not being emotionally able to "taste" sweet emotions, while still being able to experience "savory" emotions like love. It can also, as side effects, induce depression, anxiety, stress, sedation, and even frustration in me, which seem like common sense natural psychological responses to being emotionally numbed of pleasure. Eventually, I was diagnosed as also having PTSD from the mental "health" system's treatment of me over the years. Stress alone is the biggest factor in cases of schizophrenia, more so than any biological factor, according to the latest scientific research.

Just recently, I discovered by researching my genetics and alternative, complementary, and natural medicine therapies for schizophrenia, bipolar disorder, and schizoaffective disorder that I have a genetic mutation I inherited called MTHFR that affects my vitamin B absorption. It affects my system such that I have a deficiency that is not always detected by normal vitamin B level tests. It can cause depression, anxiety, irritability, fatigue, emotional numbness, cognitive and memory issues, and even mimic symptoms of schizophrenia, but it doesn't necessarily always have negative emotional or psychological effects. This explains how my real diagnosis and symptomology could go undetected, undiagnosed, even misunderstood, misinterpreted, misdiagnosed, and mislabeled until the real state of affairs was knowledgeably related to. Interestingly, my integrative medicine doctor's office told me that around a third of the population has this genetic mutation, so I have great hope and a great sense of purpose in telling my story, because it could significantly help large portions of society.

I corrected the issue at age 41 by supplementing with a special type of methylated vitamin B complex, and any residual symptoms were resolved, leaving me with just the side effects of the court-ordered, contraindicated chemical lobotomy, which has been malpractice the whole time. I can't help but laugh at the irony that the "medicine" intended to heal me is, and has been, the biggest cause of my disabled health. With my vitamin B deficiency, I think it is important to mention that the rest of my brain and central nervous system were not only functional but actually quite high functioning. In fact, the symptoms that I naturally felt when I did experience them at my baseline were similar metaphorically to the sensation of being emotionally or mentally haunted by a dead ghost. They could also be compared to looking through eyeglasses that have transparent smudges or obstructions with a fully functional sound mind. They were real, and I had a relationship with them, but my mental state was not centered or rooted in the symptoms, and I experienced a marked and insightful detachment mentally from all of the symptoms internally. This was due in part to my practice of Zen Buddhist meditation and in part because my heart, soul, spirit, the rest of my brain, central nervous system, and intuition were actually very high functioning.

The facility that tested my IQ told my mother that I was a genius and that their test was not designed to measure people as smart as me accurately. I finished the visual puzzle section of the test with a perfect score, faster than anyone ever had before at that testing facility. Most of my test results came back in the 95-99 percentile. They also said that my actual scores were higher than the test indicated, which were in their superior category for verbal intelligence at 129, very superior for combined intelligence at 132, and very superior at 142 for nonverbal intelligence. The suspected results were higher than the numbers because my comments to the facilitator during testing indicated to her that I was actually looking for some patterns bigger and more complex than the test even factored in, which inclined them to think that I could be smarter than the test itself at points.

I also system-busted the part of the exam which tests the individual's relationship with the unknown, by realizing that I didn't know and commenting while answering in an obviously randomized A, B, C, D pattern mentally as a form of strategic protest to the part of the test that invariably relied on chance and unknown validity, all while verbalizing the fact that I didn't know if I needed to know the previous unknown answers to know the current one, which again was a pattern smarter than the test was even testing for. My results exceeded Mensa's qualification requirement of scoring 130 or better on combined intelligence for that specific test, which would put me in the top 2% of IQ test results. Also, when I was in fourth grade, I had a tenth grade reading level and was reading books like Homer's The Odyssey for fun.

In addition, I have been interested in and practicing meditation and mindfulness for the majority of my adult life. When I participated in Neurofeedback sessions around age 30, after several months of sessions, I was told that normally, they would then do a peak performance session. However, it was unnecessary because I had been functioning at peak performance levels the whole time since the beginning of the treatment.

I am also certified in a variety of complementary, alternative, integrative, and natural therapies, including a Zen master meditation practitioner certificate, diplomas in Neuropsychology, Modern Applied Psychology, Parapsychology, and Holistic Herbalism, a Master Herbalist certificate, and certificates in Cognitive Behavioral Therapy and Integrative Health and Medicine. I have also earned certificates of study in Existential Psychotherapy, Advanced Level Psychology, Past Life Regression, the Psychology of Near-Death Experiences (NDE), Homeopathy, Natural Medicine, Crystal Healing, Laughter Yoga, Shaolin Qi Gong, Tai Chi, Quantum Healing, Sound Healing and Sound Therapy, Soundwave Therapy, Laughter NeuroLinguistic Programming, and Medical Cannabis Advising. I also have a certificate in Anatomy and Physiology, a certificate from Yale University in The Nature of Genius, and also a Professional Certificate from Berklee Online in General Music.

I am also in the process of studying with the University of Metaphysical Sciences toward eventually earning a Bachelor's Degree in Metaphysics, then a Master's degree in Metaphysical Science, and finally a Ph.D. in Paranormal Science and Parapsychology. I am what is known as a polymath, or in more common terms, a Renaissance man. Poly means many, and the math part of the word polymath means learned. Upon completion of my master's degree, I would be eligible to be ordained as a minister of The Wisdom of the Heart Church. The Wisdom of the Heart Church is a cross-cultural, non-denominational spiritual organization that recognizes God in everything, similar to the Sufi Mystic tradition of Islam's interpretation of the diverse manifestations, expressions, and paths of Allah's divinity. It also parallels Universalist Christians and Kabbalistic Judaism. It makes sense if you think about it, because God would obviously have the most ways to skin a cat.

On top of all the things mentioned above, when I was 18 years old in the year 2000, I experienced a spiritual awakening that led me into the inner and interconnected workings of the universe, my soul, and ultimately God, The Holy Spirit, Jesus, Allah, Brahman, Buddha Nature, The Great Spirit, the collective unconscious, and my own subconscious and superconscious. My psychologist, who is also trained in Zen and shamanism, in addition to being a licensed psychologist, thinks that I have gifts that are being misinterpreted as symptoms. My medical marijuana doctor, who is also an Osteopathic physician and general practitioner, in addition to being an International Integrative medicine expert, doesn't think that I have been schizophrenic in the 10-plus years that he has known me. The following is my attempt to chronicle my journey in hopes that it can make a positive difference in the world; however that may be.

Chapter One:

Indigo Childhood

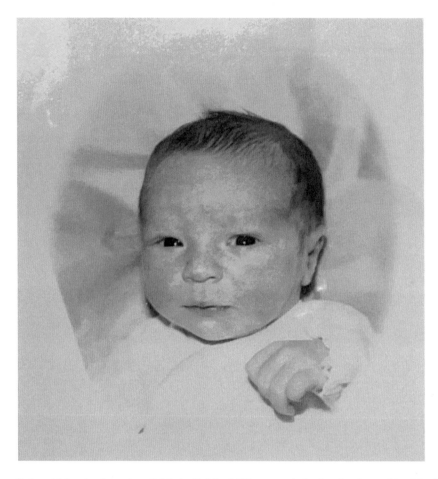

I suppose I should begin the tale of this individual life toward the beginning of it. Having already told you my birth details, and in order to give you a bit of background information and context, I will start chronologically with a brief description of my childhood and upbringing. My mother was a smart, kind, and compassionate woman who was loved by many for good reason. In high school, her superlative was most musical, and she graduated a year early from high school before attending Fitchburg State College for accounting later. She raised me to embody kindness, and to trust my gut intuition. She was historically the softie, while my dad tended to be the disciplinarian figure. My father was an intelligent student-athlete at Dartmouth College around the time of my birth, and after graduating, he later went on to become a systems engineer for Raytheon.

He is the oldest of a big Sicilian and Irish family of seven children. He was raised in America after his ancestors immigrated here from Italy a couple of generations ago. His upbringing was by a strict Roman

Catholic Deacon in my grandfather, which I'm pretty sure was reflected in my father's strong, silent type, or critically yelling parenting style. I should note that he is equally as strict with himself, if not more so. He is an excellent provider with a superb work ethic and moral compass, despite having been a workaholic to the extent that it ended his first marriage to my mother. His example taught me the value of self discipline, a solid work ethic, and of my own ability to be mentally tough as nails when necessary. Teammates on his adult recreational softball teams would even call him "Miracle" because of his extraordinary athletic feats. My family used to have little joke celebrations on the rare occasions that he was found to be wrong, because he was almost always right if he dared open his mouth in the first place. I am the oldest child of three siblings, with a sister who is a year and a half younger than me and a brother who is seven years younger.

I have great relationships with my brother and sister. My sister is a total sweetheart and a great mother to a family of 5 children, including two adopted brothers. They call me Uncle Donut affectionately because I would frequently get donuts for the kids when I slept over. My brother is a realistic perfectionist, creative writing professor, and musical genius, in my opinion. Just to give a bit of foreshadowing, I grew into becoming what I refer to as the Psychedelic Sheep of my family.

In my early years, my family moved around New England every year until I reached third grade, when we spent two consecutive years in Andover, Massachusetts. My parents had spent significant portions of their upbringing in Andover, but it had become much more affluent since the days of their youth. As a result, I vividly remember being ganged up on and ridiculed by a large circle of children at recess for having L.A. Gear air-pump-up sneakers, which were all that my family could afford and apparently were too cheap compared to the Reebok and Nike name-brand options that were popular amongst the children at that time.

I was already a shy child by nature, and by being nurtured repeatedly as the new kid at school, so I was devastated that the kids could be so cruel about sneakers that I was actually very excited to own. I had a hard time fitting in, and repeatedly pretended to be sick so that I could stay home from school and avoid the bullies and boredom of a curriculum that did not match my mental capacity or potential. I was a fairly sensitive child emotionally, and at one point in my early years, I wanted to prove to myself that I was still tough. Accordingly, I proceeded to get a dental cavity filled at an appointment without using Novacaine or any numbing agent. I didn't flinch a millimeter or cry, so I was quite proud of myself after having been reduced to tears by my peers previously.

Recognizing that I was deeply unhappy there, my family was kind enough to pack up one more time to try to find a home somewhere else where I could thrive better. This led us to move to Merrimac, Massachusetts when I was entering fifth grade. It was a small town with a regionalized middle and high school that was one of the top public schools in the state and country at the time. We remained in Merrimac through my high school graduation, when I left home for Burlington, Vermont, to attend The University of Vermont as an art major.

In Merrimac, I eventually found several circles of different friends, and by high school, I was particularly close to at least one member of almost every social circle. I was an athlete who played multiple sports, with soccer being my sport of choice until I found snowboarding, skateboarding, hacky sack, and frisbee. I was voted co-captain of my varsity soccer team my senior year in my third year on the successful varsity team, though late in the season, they took the title of co-captain away from me because I got caught smoking a cigarette. I graduated National Honor Society with a 1400 on my SAT split 690/710. I also achieved high marks on the Chemistry and Writing SAT IIs and my MCAS test. My two superlatives in the school newspaper my senior year were "Most likely to get in a fight with a teacher" and "Least likely to do his homework."

That was due to the fact that I almost never did my homework because I would ace all of the tests and projects without even studying, and would frequently question and critique some of the dogmatic practices and outdated curriculum of the various teachers that did not factor in advanced students like myself. I was oftentimes kept off of the honor and high honor rolls because of my unsatisfactory marks in the effort category, despite earning grades that otherwise qualified me for high honors most quarters. My family used to compare me to the character Kramer from the show Seinfeld, in part because of my eccentric nature and also, conveniently enough, because when I teased my mushroom bowl cut of the day up, my wavy brown hair even visually resembled Kramer's.

Passionate debates on topics like religion, in particular, were commonplace at my family dinners growing up. My genetic background is diverse, containing Sicilian and Irish on both sides, Greek, Balkan, Spanish/Portuguese, Scottish, English, Northwestern European, Scandinavian, Ashkenazi Jewish, Levantine, Egyptian, Arabic, Northern Chinese and Tibetan, and even some Neanderthal genes. So, while I was often shy and reserved socially, I also had a deeply passionate side to me that would come to the surface depending on the company and context. My father was Roman Catholic, and my mother got confirmed as a Christian around the time that I decided not to get confirmed, after attending church and Sunday school for my entire life leading up to that. My brother attended a private Christian high school, and both my brother and sister attended the same Christian undergraduate college, where my sister studied to become a youth minister, and my brother went on to get a master's degree in creative writing at another graduate school.

Meanwhile, I was extremely scientific in my approach and perspective, very grounded, and skeptical about fanciful religious concepts for which I needed evidence. I was still very open-minded about spiritual concepts in general, but I tended not to take an orthodox approach to religion, mostly because so much of pop

21

religion seemed dogmatic to me. I took it upon myself to make sure that my younger siblings did not turn into religious bigots like many who immerse themselves deeply into a single religion can unfortunately become, despite the tragic irony of that.

At the age of sixteen, I started experimenting with tobacco, marijuana, alcohol, and even occasionally psychedelic mushrooms. By the age of seventeen, I was pretty much already a young stoner, regularly smoking herb before school to help make the dull environment more emotionally tolerable. I had begun to try to address some social anxiety and depression issues that had become more prominent in high school with a combination of mindfulness and self-medication. Don't get me wrong, I also used those substances recreationally at the time, but in a sense, even the recreational use had therapeutic aspects to it, too.

I found tobacco to be helpful with stress relief and focus, and alcohol helped shy, reserved Nick be more of a light-hearted social butterfly and have fun. Marijuana helped with my depression and my anxiety. The mushrooms were great for me spiritually and also provided me with some of my first peer-validated experiences with intuition, interconnectedness, and oneness.

It was around this time in my life when I started feeling like there was something deeply wonderful about the universe that was waiting to be unveiled. I was beginning to catch glimpses of something greater, and one of my girlfriends senior year was a hippie, so I was being exposed to some high-minded ideals regularly. I decided to follow my heart to be immersed in the hippie culture that was so pervasive in Burlington, Vermont, where this young Psychonaut could blossom into the psychedelic sheep that was drawn to that path seeking higher consciousness, wisdom, heart, and soul.

Chapter Two:

Coming of Age

My freshman year of college starting in the fall of 2000 was a bit of a whirlwind, and was the beginning of what amounted to an epic adventure for my soul and spirit. Enculturating myself by choice in an atmosphere of open-minded progressiveness that had a deep respect for classic cultural notions like love, freedom, and reverence for peace, I was finally thriving by my own definitions. Instead of choosing my social options from a cliquey, narrow menu, I finally felt like I had my pick of the social litter from more options than I could possibly manifest into reality. I was a social butterfly at parties and in my local dormitory subcultures, making more friends than names I could remember.

It might be noteworthy that at the time, the University of Vermont was ranked one of the top 10 party schools in the nation, a fact that I was well aware of and deliberately factored in. Having been denied admission to several Ivy League universities, I had been offered free tuition at any Massachusetts state university based on my state standardized test scores, yet I consciously sought the social atmosphere of Burlington, Vermont. Presented with the option to socialize or go to class, I frequently accepted a reduction in my final grade for classes because of my lack of homework and attendance, while getting grades good enough just by acing the tests after reading the textbooks the day before. That let me spend my time instead playing music, socializing with some of the greatest people that I have ever met, and diving deeper and deeper into my spiritual self and my meditation practice.

At the very beginning of my freshman year at college, I discovered the book Zen Flesh Zen Bones, which, if Zen had a Bible, would be it. However, Zen wouldn't have a Bible, which the book even establishes. I read it cover to cover swiftly, and then throughout the year, I would go through the entire book item by item, choosing one parable, kōan, or meditation to meditate on for every day of my freshman year following until I had meditated upon every facet of the book extensively. I was enthralled and felt like something about it resonated with me more deeply than any other philosophy, religion, or spiritual phenomena I had encountered previously. I would spend hours in small groups with friends, playing music in drum circles and impromptu guitar jam sessions, listening to music, playing hacky sack, and frequently smoking cannabis, all while meditating.

Cannabis, being classified as a hypnotic drug, can help to put the brain into what is known in neuroscience as Theta brain states. Theta states are also used during hypnosis and deep meditative states, as well as occurring at the outer boundaries of human sleep before and after falling asleep. They are commonly experienced by the masses when driving with a wandering mind, only to reach a destination and not be able to remember how they got there. It is in these deeper brain states that we can scientifically access and interact with the subconscious. Interestingly enough, one time, while under the influence of anesthesia in high school, waking up right after surgery, I gave my witnessing mother a quite in-depth and enthusiastic sermon about the merits of meditation years before I was ever exposed to any meditation literature or culture, a conversation which I do not consciously remember to this day, but was told about by her years later.

During the autumn of my freshman year at UVM, I continued my explorations into what psychedelics had to offer. I had begun to approach them as a spiritual tool for experiencing altered states of consciousness, in an effort to evolve my consciousness into its highest potential. I expanded my consciousness in a spiritually directed manner with mushrooms, AMT (a relative of DMT), and LSD. I eventually reached a peak in my state of consciousness during the first night that I tried acid. The night left a vivid impression on me and represented a milestone in the evolution and progress of my soul. I think that it is worth describing because it helped to lay some of the foundations for my personality as a grown adult of my own making, and was all at once the beginning, mountaintop, and first time coming full circle for my spiritual spiral journey along the path.

So, the night of my first acid trip, there was a Phil Lesh show in town. Phil Lesh is one of the original members of The Grateful Dead, who were well known for their experimental and progressive use of psychedelics. Accordingly, a friend of a friend had obtained a vile of the most potent type of liquid acid, known as L-25, from the show. A bunch of my friends and I decided that we would like to try some that night, and my immediate circle of friends all started with a small dose to see how we felt. After ingesting my initial one drop of liquid acid and waiting an hour, I was disappointed that I was not feeling any different yet.

I decided to go back for more, but when the supplier went to drop one additional drop onto my palm from the Sweet Breath container that had the LSD in it, he squeezed it too hard by mistake and immediately said, "Oops," as what hippies refer to as a "puddle" of 5-7 drops ran up one wrinkle in my palm and down another. I figured that since I wasn't feeling anything after one drop, a relatively veteran psilocybin user like myself could handle that amount and might need more, so I quickly lapped up the puddle enthusiastically with my tongue. A while passed, and I still wasn't feeling any different. My friends and the supplier, however, were feeling significant effects.

The supplier was actually doing something referred to as Candy Flippin' in that subculture, which consists of ingesting LSD and Ecstasy (or MDMA) at the same time. I do not know how much of either he was on because I had barely gotten his first name so far, but apparently, he had taken too much and was beginning to show signs of that. First, he stripped down naked outdoors right in the middle of our campus dorms in a public, populated area and started running around with his arms outstretched, yelling, "Is this turbo

24

world?! Are we all dead?!" My friends saw this, and some of them went to try to help deal with the scene he was making, while many of the others felt that they were in a fragile state of mind from the acid and decided to leave in an effort to find a more soothing environment to be in.

The next thing I knew, after about a half hour had gone by, I saw a commotion building up. I was told that the supplier having the bad trip had assaulted one of the girls in the dorm upstairs, and there was a large crowd of drunken frat boy types and jocks eagerly assembling in the stairwell, preparing to beat him up for it.

I pleaded with the angry mob that the young man was under the influence of heavy drugs and didn't even know the difference currently between death and life, so any hopes of teaching him a lesson somehow would be in vain. I asked that someone please call an ambulance and get him a shot of Thorazine and medical help instead of beating him up. They proceeded to get him an ambulance and professional attention instead of their proposed violence. I, on the other hand, after about 3 hours from my initial dose, still wasn't feeling any different, which was starting to actually make me wonder, considering how the same substance had brought another veteran user over the edge into such a bad trip.

About an hour later, I witnessed a reddish streak of what I perceived as energy of some sort that was not visible to the naked visual eyes, but was being witnessed by my mind's eye or third eye. This was the first time in my life that I had visibly seen any type of energy, Chi, or spirit, which was frequently described in detail by the hippie, stoner, and new age subcultures that I had been hanging out with, and by Eastern mystics, Yogis, Buddhists, and Hindus. The notion of Satan occurred to me at this point, which was my first experience with anything demonic in this incarnation, though I got the distinct impression that there was still an angelic element to it. I was in a state of intuitive knowing, coupled with a mental skepticism because of the LSD that I had taken earlier, despite not having any other noticeable auditory or visual hallucinations yet that night. I intuitively sensed that there was an extremely evil and dangerous component spiritually to the disembodied energy that I was witnessing. I retired momentarily to re-center myself and distance myself to safety from whatever negative psychic energy I seemed to be perceiving.

I sought refuge upstairs in my dorm room, where I proceeded to have my only vision of the night that I knew was purely in my mind's eye. As I gazed into the big mirror on the back of my dorm room door, I saw a fixed image of myself in the reflection. It was colored like some type of static artwork that I could examine. My head and face were made up of black and white areas with yellow outlines, and surrounding my head were what appeared to be meaningful icons and symbols. I had the distinct impression that I was looking at a sort of spiritual map of my soul, with different images representing different aspects of myself from not only this life but also a rich historical blueprint of my very old soul, which I was consciously reconnecting with for the first time.

There was an art palette that I first consciously associated with being a historical Renaissance man, because I had the feeling that I had also been an architect. There was an ink pen that I associated with writing as a purpose in not only this life but past lives too, and an acoustic guitar that I felt connected to in this life and past ones. Then, before I had time to consciously examine all of the hundred or so images surrounding me, which seemed to be made out of Chi or spiritual light, I got the distinct impression that I had been a shipbuilder in a past life. I just knew it. The next thing I noticed was an icon in the upper right-hand side of my reflection that looked like a naked indigo body of light, or Chi, standing straight up with arms outstretched to the sides and a heart chakra green circular aura around it. The image reminded me of Christ, The Holy Spirit, and of yet-to-be-uncovered relationships with Christianity and Tai Chi that my soul has had from past lives.

It was at this point that my mind wandered, and I realized that if the universe is all one holistic entity, then we are all one and communing with Jesus and the Holy Spirit, Holy Ghost, Trinity, God, Allah, Buddha Nature, Brahman, or whatever you want to call the Universal macrocosm and its diverse individual manifestations. Evidence for a unified interconnectedness can be found scientifically in the fact that everything in the universe is quantum entangled. It was my first experience with what The New Age Movement refers to as Christ Consciousness. Instantaneously, I reminded myself that this didn't mean that I was specifically Jesus and that, in fact, I was a different soul altogether from the historical individual known as Jesus in his incarnation around 2,000 years ago, scoffing somewhat at the very notion.

I then had a vivid sense of nostalgia for what appeared to be the tip of the iceberg of my old soul that reached far below the surface consciousness into the deepest depths of my subconscious and being. Next, I had an experience of universal acceptance of myself and others, which was deeply profound. I realized that as long as I could live with myself honestly, I was destined to live a fulfilling life. The rest of the night was rather uneventful for me, which paradoxically hardened the sense of reality and intuitive knowing that I was experiencing, all while I couldn't help but question the validity of my own experience because of the nature of what had transpired that night. Having reached a spiritual pinnacle, I felt that from there on in, I wanted to only use psychedelics like psilocybin and LSD sparingly, if not avoiding them completely for the most part. I had heard Salvador Dali quoted as saying, "My mind is drugs," and I sought to achieve any altering of my consciousness via meditation and naturally occurring brain states and states of mind, perhaps with the help of some tobacco or cannabis, which I had begun to approach as sacraments. Much later in life, I heard stories of Eastern mystics and gurus who were also relatively unphased by hallucinogens, which seemed to resonate and validate my own experience in hindsight. My favorite thing to do when trippin' on mushrooms previously was to control my own visualizations, which I had never even heard of people experiencing.

Soon after, I began working on a poem and an illustration of it, which described the experience for me. Despite being involved in visual arts for my whole life, and even winning an award at the world renowned Wang Center in Boston as a high school student, I had primarily been a photorealistic artist without a vivid

26

imagination. After the night on LSD, however, despite having such a surprisingly minuscule amount of visualizations that night, I found that I could envision complex, multiple-entendre imagery that even bordered on surreal optical illusions effortlessly. I would stare at a blank page and meditate, projecting my mental image onto the page like tracing paper, with muscle memory, physical skill, hand-eye coordination, and mastery from a life in the arts to manifest my imagery exactly how I intended to. I felt like I had finally mastered my craft as an art form, in addition to a skill set of techniques. Following is a picture of the 14" x 17" pencil drawing I created to describe my experience that night, which I titled Glassid, along with the poem it helps to illustrate. Parts of the drawing were made by expelling my subconscious, other parts on psychedelic mushrooms, and others utilizing meditation. I started to get bored with art and became more interested in the spiritual aspects of life.

Glassid

One drop turns into two or more, reality drips out the door.

One spark ignites the drops that drip,

And Satan's coming for the trip.

My mind looks out his windowpane,

To watch the sunset turn to rain,

The colors seep into my brain,

And leave a rippling mental stain.

Your face contorts clearer through Alice's mirror.

The wrinkles in my brain leak through my pores like acid rain,

While a second's revelation bullies hours of contemplation.

Losing myself to thoughts on a shelf,

Lost in a maze of fluorescent haze,

The clarity grips me as hindrance is set free.

Possibility's range grows ever so strange,

Lost in a gaze, winding maze of my ways,

Every twist was a turn,

How they shine, how they burn.

How true can one world really be,

Until it's been fictitious?

How blind can one man be to see,

That sound seems so delicious.

How good can one man wholly be,

Not having been malicious?

How free can your mind really feel,

'Til it's seen your subconscious?

How open can a spirit be while closed in by a wall?

How tall can one man really stand until they've seen him fall?

How comforting is it to think you walk instead of crawl?

How telling it can be to see that it's not it at all.

The days the grass is always green,

And sound remains to me unseen,

Seem distant, cold, and spiritless,

When faced with this new fiery mess.

But if you look instead of see,

Then caged your mind will always be,

So come and see, you won't look back,

The mirror's false without the crack.

After experiencing what felt like a moment of enlightenment and both a climax and rebirth as part of my spiritual awakening that fateful night, I invested my time and effort with renewed vigor in the cultural environment that was so good at fostering that type of experience. Burlington, Vermont was somewhat of a New Age Atlantis combined with a hippie Mecca, and a Rastafarian Zion at the time. It was full of conscious, awake spirits, souls, and minds. There was a certain air of transformation, actualization, and spiritual evolution that was commonplace in the community and fostered an atmosphere with predominantly great vibes, intellectual curiosity and investigation, and spiritual growth, and it was very nurturing.

I was enthralled by the various spiritual and subcultural ideas of interconnectedness, idealism, and the down-to-earth and naturalistic applications of the people's approaches and methodologies for integrating advanced religious and spiritual concepts into practical, everyday type of manifestations. Most of the people there really did "Think globally, Act locally." I was trying to approach all of these big, important concepts with an open mind as I explored them, but also with a rigorously scientific methodology and logical philosophical perspective.

I couldn't help but entertain a healthy level of skepticism for some of the ideas involved, since they were the early stages of my exposure to many of them in any realistically achievable form in this incarnation of mine. Also, because many of the suppositions, attitudes, and ideas were not only rejected but even condemned by the mainstream Western pop culture in which I had been raised, so I had been enculturated to approach them with skepticism, if not even disdain. I intensely investigated psychic phenomena in particular.

It started with an experience of telepathy that a group of friends and I had in high school during a psilocybin session that we all experienced, verbalized, and validated. By the time I was halfway through freshman year of college, I had started to take mental notes of all of the times that I had known what someone was going to say before they said it to evaluate the data for statistical significance. After a few months, the large volume of data was enough to make me lose count once it got into the hundreds of times, having become a commonplace event in my life by then. I also routinely and regularly discussed telepathic experiences with many different people and friends from many different social circles I encountered, with an overwhelming amount of positive correlations and validation.

At this point in my life, I was sure that even if the average American Joe and Jane Doe didn't accept these types of phenomena, they were very real and externally validated repeatedly across significant demographics of the populations I was surrounded by, including my own experiences. There was clearly a combination of such a sheer large amount of occurrences, and also enough specifically significant data to disprove that it was all coincidence or chance, or even explainable by commonly accepted paradigms of Western pop culture science.

Chapter Three:

Shamanic Calling

For the rest of my freshman year, I continued my meditation practice intensely, meditating on the problems of the world and what I was going to do to address them. I picked up the acoustic guitar at age 18, after a lifetime of singing in the shower, in the car, in church choirs, and in school choruses. I took basic music classes in elementary school and even studied cello for a year in fourth grade, but stopped music classes and choruses in high school. I was deeply invested in teaching myself how to play guitar so that I could combine it with my singing and the insights I gained through meditation in an offering of wise, poetic lyrics in song format that could be constructive and productive while also entertaining. I had already dabbled a bit in writing poetry starting in high school, so lyrics seemed like a natural transition and evolution.

I was hoping to get good enough at music to make a significant contribution toward many of the social and psychological problems and issues facing civilization in these turbulent times. Accordingly, I skipped a lot of classes to play music with friends and meditate on the world's problems and potential constructive avenues for progress that I could address using my music as a form of medicine. As a result, in conjunction with the vitamin B deficiency that I mentioned earlier, unknown to me at the time, while my mental state was very clear and high functioning, at the same time, the sheer magnitude of the world's problems I was routinely confronting in my meditations weighed heavily on my heart, head, and soul.

By the end of the school year, I had filed with the school's mental health department seeking some help for symptoms of depression and distractedness, which were interfering with my studies. I left for a summer vacation in Bar Harbor, staying with friends after a breakup with my beautiful artist ex-girlfriend, who told me that I "was the type of guy she would want to marry in like five years because I was perfect." Unfortunately for me, she needed space for herself in the meantime, so we were separated after an intense and very deeply committed and loving relationship for the majority of the previous school year.

The following summer, I was prescribed 45 milligrams of Adderall daily after answering a brief questionnaire that supposedly qualified me for a diagnosis of ADD. The Adderall, while it did increase my focus and attention, frequently made me feel very jittery and overstimulated. I even believe that it may have induced some social anxiety and occasional panic attacks combined with the still undiscovered vitamin B deficiency. I was, on the one hand, trying to live my best possible life and coping, but on the other hand, being crippled by complicating my preexisting condition with high doses of amphetamine salt that was being prescribed to me erroneously. Fed up with my situation and hungry for answers and solutions, I turned back to the system, which had now made a tangibly bad first impression on me, for more thorough testing.

I was reluctant to seek help from a mental health system that frowned openly and even aggressively upon many aspects of the subcultures that I had become accustomed to. Still, I figured that at least getting tested might provide some valuable insight. In my opinion, categorizing oneness experiences as oceanic psychotic features like pop Western psychiatry does is quite obviously biased cultural bigotry. The population of Eastern cultures where psychic phenomena are considered normal is immensely large and in the billions, compared to the relatively small population of Western "scientists" who are subjectively biasing their definitions of illness based on only their own ignorant cultural norms. I went to a psychological evaluation facility in North Andover, Massachusetts, seeking to have my mental, intellectual, and emotional status tested. That is the facility that told my mother I was a genius, and on their IQ test, I performed way above the averages in almost every category. There were two categories in which I performed significantly lower, however.

In the average processing speed category, I was only in the 50th percentile, which I attributed in part to being more thorough than even the test was, combined with my propensity to meditate, smoke pot, my naturally easygoing demeanor, and in hindsight, may have been affected by my yet unknown, undiagnosed, and untreated vitamin B deficiency. I also was not aware that the test was even being timed, so I wasn't in a rush. It did seem to validate my friend's high school nickname for me, however, which was Mirislowla.

The other category was my attention span results, which were in the 80th percentile range. They said that I had what they called a perceived attention deficit because my attention span results weren't in the upper 95-99th percentile range that the rest of my intellectual faculties functioned at. So technically, I had reasonably high-functioning, above average attention span results, and in fact, I did not actually have Attention Deficit Disorder.

They also said that emotionally, I had what they called at the time Mixed Mood Aphasia. I attributed this mixed state to the fact that in my efforts to be conscious, on point, and mindful, I was frequently aware of both sides of every coin and even, as I say comically, the rim job. This meant that I was frequently in a state of mixed emotions, a muddy gray compromise, or questioning even my own emotional state. I felt like this description fit me perfectly at the time, and I wasn't honestly convinced that it was even avoidable for a big-picture thinker like myself.

I went back to school in Burlington at the end of the summer, feeling like I pretty much had myself figured out so far to an extent. After playing guitar and singing on the streets and at several open mics around Burlington, I was offered my first paid music gig, playing two sets at a welcome-back outdoor concert at The University of Vermont. I was psyched, and despite not practicing at all as a group with any of the musicians whom I invited to play with me on stage, we impressed the headliner's manager enough just by improvising for him to have a mutual friend let me know that he was interested in booking me for a New England tour. I had only been playing guitar for a year or so and only writing songs for about 6 months, so I decided to pass on the opportunity. It was a promising start, but the perfectionist in me wanted to hone my craft more before taking it to the next level.

I enrolled in the fall of my sophomore year at UVM, starting a new program as a music major. I went into it very passionate and excited, but was quickly bored and didn't fit well with the formal education setting for music there. I preferred to play by ear, from the heart, with my soul, and creatively in the spirit of my emotions. I felt like the academic approach to music was abstract, dry, and overly technical for my style. I detested reading sheet music and learning how to play a bunch of songs that I didn't even like on a bunch of instruments that I had no desire to play, so I decided to drop out and reevaluate my path back home at my parents' house in Merrimac and take a semester off instead.

At this point, I read a book that made a distinctly vivid impact on my life. It was called The Handbook to Higher Consciousness. It was an old book from the 60s or 70s that I found in a used bookstore. It described treating your consciousness kind of like a symbolic computer, with programmable software that could be self-manipulated with mindful intent. It also delved into some of the more logical and practical aspects of higher states of consciousness that I was exploring on my own and in the company of friends. I was also beginning to expand my meditation practice to include affirmations, trance states, and self-hypnosis as tools for character development and therapeutic interventions.

At this time in my life, I also became increasingly interested in Native American spirituality and cross-cultural definitions of Shamanism. I read anthropologist Carlos Castenada's accounts of Don Juan, which I felt intrigued by and drawn to. It reached the point where I had a calling of sorts to make shamanism a part of my life. I wanted to learn to heal with my music as medicine and potentially get much deeper into the spiritual and intuitive aspects of shamanism, which already held so much appeal for me. I started to view my first night on acid as a type of vision quest retrospectively. In many Shamanic traditions, a Shaman has a calling. They are then overtaken by an illness so that they can learn to heal themselves and are, after that, equipped with the knowledge and ability to heal others. I didn't know it then, but this shift in my soul would eventually prove to bring my spirit through ego death and rebirth yet again, even more intensely along my soul's spiral path with higher highs and lower lows each time, and would redirect my purpose and meaning of life immensely. I hope that even this book and story can function as medicine for society and possibly help people to heal psychologically, spiritually, scientifically, and culturally.

Chapter Four:

Adventures in Karma

I returned to The University of Vermont in the spring of my sophomore year, living in a dorm room with one of my best friends. He was a very open-minded Indian Muslim hippie who was studying world religions, and we frequently had very in-depth philosophical discussions about religions, God, spirituality, and society. Eventually, he would introduce me to Islamic Sufism, which is a mystical branch of Islam that recognizes the divinity of Allah in all of its diverse manifestations. Immersed in such a curious atmosphere, Burlington and UVM had begun to bring out the philosopher in me much more vividly. In my freshman year, my advisor was the head of the philosophy department and also my teacher for a special small philosophy class called Rationality and Belief in God. He got to know me well, and we had an excellent rapport as kindred philosophers through many papers read and written and countless in-person discussions. My final paper for the class compared belief in God with belief in Santa Claus. I was exploring the option of creating my own major in Cognitive Science with him. He made a special exception for me because I was excelling in the philosophy class with him in the first semester, and he let me enroll in a senior-level philosophy class on The Nature of Consciousness with a guest professor from MIT in the second semester of my freshman year.

So, when I got back to school in the spring of my sophomore year, I was also heavily considering the possible path of becoming a professional philosopher, whether as a professor myself or just writing books and papers on my philosophies. I was still taking art classes at school but was getting more and more bored by required classes that were geared toward much more basic and uninformed art students than me. I wasn't taking any music classes at school, but I was steadily making progress in teaching myself and diligently practicing routinely.

I decided to dreadlock my hair at this point and spent many hours playing hacky sack, frisbee, skateboarding, snowboarding, and smoking cannabis. I had begun to approach many different activities from a meditative perspective and found that I enjoyed them much more when I did. I had also started to approach hacky sack, skateboarding, snowboarding, and dancing as forms of jazzy, practical, expressive Tai Chi. Often, the effects of cannabis were profoundly conducive to meditative states and activities, so I was, needless to say, smoking quite a bit of Ganja regularly. As long as I can remember, Vermont has had a reputation for having some of the best marijuana in the country and the world. The students used to host a peaceful protest outside the library of UVM every year on 4/20, where thousands would gather from around the country to smoke cannabis openly. April 20 of my sophomore year, however, the administration decided to put an end to the previously successful protests by substituting with a school-run concert on the library green on 4/20.

They wisely got the band Gov't Mule to play, which was a crowd appeaser, but there was a significant police presence, and they were not letting anyone possess or smoke marijuana there. The student population was deeply unsettled by the imposed end of what had become a yearly tradition, and students organized a peaceful protest on the green in the middle of the campus where my dorm was to try to keep the tradition alive.

I awoke that morning to discover that there had been a small tremor of an earthquake during the night, and that morning, while smoking herb, an ember burnt a heart-shaped hole in my cargo shorts. I went to the concert for a while, played some hacky sack, and then made my way back to my campus dorm green. I spent the afternoon philosophizing with the abundant police from local towns and even state cops while a large crowd gathered on the green. As 4:20 PM approached, there was great anticipation about whether or not to smoke cannabis in the face of the police, who were dead set on not allowing it.

As I philosophized with the students and nearby officers, there was a misunderstanding. The officer I was philosophizing with, who another officer was videotaping with a flashing red light on the camera, told me to "*Stop inciting*," which struck me as an odd and inflammatory way to refer to me philosophizing, so I said back to him something to the effect of "*Inciting?* This is a peaceful protest, and it's not like we're going to riot." Apparently, that was like saying bomb in an airport to them, and I immediately heard a voice come over his walkie-talkie saying, "Get him out of here." They then restrained my arms and started marching me through the crowd to a cruiser on the outskirts of the area.

To my surprise, one of the students with a dorm room window on the edge of the green started blasting Rage Against The Machine's version of the song *Fuck the Police* very loudly. I remember the scene like it was yesterday. I was processed and let go after some time and charged with disorderly conduct. That night, the ticker tape at the bottom of the news on CNN even mentioned the one arrest made at the UVM protest. I went down to the court office before my trial and asked for the police videotape to be entered as evidence of my innocence. They responded that the camera had malfunctioned, so there was no video. That seemed very suspicious to me, and soon after, I told the story to a friend who happened to know someone who was recording the incident on their cell phone camera as it happened. I obtained a copy of the video and entered it as evidence before my trial, and sure enough, they decided to drop the charges without even taking me to court.

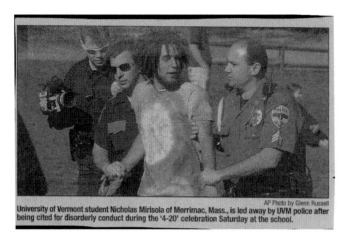

AP Photo by Glenn Russell

University of Vermont student Nicholas Mirisola of Merrimac, Mass., is led away by UVM police after being cited for disorderly conduct during the '4-20' celebration Saturday at the school.

I had been developing an interest in the historical figure Siddhartha and his different teachings in my young adulthood. My dear friend introduced me to the concept of a Dharma Bum that he had picked up from a novel by Jack Kerouac titled The Dharma Bums. My personal interpretation of the phrase involves abiding by the universal law, or Dharma, in a way so well that it provides you with what you need, in conjunction with a Buddhist-style mental aesthetic. I was very interested in this idea because it resonated with the fact that the Buddha sent his disciples out into the world as beggars. If you think about it, Jesus may have been one of the greatest Dharma Bums ever, and I mean that as a supreme compliment. I decided to try my hand at it the summer of my sophomore year, and figured a voluntary summer of homelessness and couch surfing could be a character-building experience. It was, and it turned out to be one of the most fun-loving and carefree summers of my entire life.

It was simultaneously one of the most challenging and rewarding things to try to keep my karma so good that it provided me with everything that I needed. It also involved a much more simplistic, contented mindset where even the barest necessities became a beautiful blessing, while anything beyond the bare necessities was a manifestation of abundance. I had begun to be inspired by prolific singer-songwriter Jewel's story of living out of her car and being discovered at an open mic night. She had also been a role model for me since I discovered her in my youth for her heart, soul, and emotional wisdom, which I was so happy to see in pop culture, in the face of some rather corrupted norms of society at the time.

I figured if she could do that, I could put my spin on something akin to it. She later developed into one of my mental health heroes, too, and I only wish that more pop culture promoted people with conscious, enlightening messages like her, so I set out to do whatever part I could about it. I decided to enroll at Maine College of Art in Portland for the fall of my junior year but only stayed for a semester because I was getting bored by uninspiring prerequisite classes and wanted to invest more thoroughly in my musical aspirations, which still had plenty of room to grow.

Chapter Five:

Connecting To

A Higher Power

I returned to Burlington in the spring of my junior year, but this time as a student of an independently designed interdisciplinary program at Burlington College instead of UVM. I was taking a variety of art, film, and philosophical classes that I had handpicked. I was also living in my first apartment room of my own with some friends, and had developed a wonderful romantic relationship with a stunning and charismatic lady who lived upstairs from me. I was learning about Carl Jung's theories of Transpersonal Psychology, The Collective Unconscious, and shadow and archetype philosophies. I was also beginning to explore and experiment with group and collective consciousness, as well as my theories about what I was referring to as the Superconscious.

It is like the opposite of the subconscious; it is over our heads instead of deep down inside, and it can access and interact with the collective consciousness and collective unconscious. I later learned that the heart, which is 60% nerve cells and the fifth center of the central nervous system, functions as the conscious tip of the superconscious iceberg and is the center of our being where the superconscious, subconscious, and conscious converge. I began to work on a pen drawing for class, unbeknownst to me how profoundly it would impact my life at the start of it.

I didn't usually make rough drafts for my artwork, preferring to mentally work in my head until I knew what I wanted to create. I set out on my newest project with some concepts in mind that I wanted to integrate and apply to the artwork. I had been a long-time fan of fractals, the mathematical phenomenon that incorporate self-similarity, infinite scalability, and imaginary numbers. I wanted to incorporate the element of fractals conceptually by drawing a large turtle or tortoise eye with a repeating skin scale pattern that was made up of an optical illusion that either looked like a peyote lotus abstract flower with leaves or a pair of eyes with a peyote lotus blossom where the third eye would be, depending on how you perceived it.

It was visually supposed to be a form of a Buddhist Mandala, too. In the iris, I drew a repeating pattern of humans with their arms outstretched and touching hands forming prayer poses in a ring, with hearts of energy filling the spaces between them. For the reflection on the pupil, I wanted to try something experimental for the first time. I had never previously attempted to do so, but this time, if it was meant to be, I was going to offer myself as a medium for the superconscious to draw whatever it wanted. I entered a meditative state, stilled my mind, and mentally offered myself as an instrument to be puppeteered by the superconscious. I queried what the problems of society are as an inspirational theme for that portion of the drawing.

Sure enough, through no conscious will of my own, my hand started drawing a surreal combination of evocative imagery while my mind sat in awe. There were images of a horned demon berating a plump bald man, a swastika, a computer, an upside-down hand holding money, a naked woman with legs spread wide open, and more, all organized in a manner that either could be perceived as the shape of a tree, or a mushroom cloud from a nuclear explosion, depending on how you looked at it, like an optical illusion. I gave the final 14" x 17" copy to a friend as a gift before I ever had a chance to make a duplicate or record of it, but I was even once asked if I had made it using a computer, though it was entirely by hand with a pen and no rough draft.

I was smitten by this, and over the next year or so, I studied books independently like The Biology of Transcendence by Joseph Chilton Pearce, The Tao Te Ching, The Science of Being and The Art of Living by Maharishi Mahesh Yogi, The Sense of Being Stared at and Other Aspects of the Extended Mind by Rupert Sheldrake, a book titled The Tao of Physics, and a book about the holographic nature of reality, among others. The Biology of Transcendence taught me about the heart's bioenergetics aura called a Torah, which is holographic and universal. The Tao Te Ching by Lao Tzu was an invaluable resource and inspiration about the basic theme of all of my spiritual pursuits, the title of which translates to The Way of Virtue.

Maharishi Mahesh Yogi taught me transcendental meditation, which I was immediately drawn to integrate into my meditative practice. Rupert Sheldrake's book taught me that the most informed parapsychologists have repeatedly found statistically significant scientific results when testing humans and animals for extrasensory perception. It was much more valid than mainstream pop science had erroneously and dogmatically made it out to be.

The Holographic Nature of Reality book was very compelling scientific theories about the self-evident self-similarity found in the universe, which I found complemented the philosophical and spiritual components of my perspective thus far. The Tao of Physics really connected all of the dots between the Eastern, spiritual, and mystic perspectives that I was heavily invested in and the parallels with modern science and quantum mechanics. I also did some research on group consciousness, which revealed that when scientists slow down the frame rate when filming flocks of birds in flight or schools of fish swimming, it is not possible to tell which one moves first. This means that they are synchronized in a collectively coherent manner.

Filled with curiosity, I started to experiment with long-distance telepathy, group consciousness, and surrendering to what, at that point, felt vaguely like a higher power. One time, while sitting with a pen in hand

and an open journal, in an automatic writing session, I scribbled out the words "I am spirit controlled, soul knowing, mind over matter" with no conscious effort on my part. At this point in my life, surrounded by like-minded individuals, small-group telepathic experiences and spiritual phenomena were normal. In fact, you were the outsider, abnormal, and in the dark if you did not sense or experience this too.

I started to experiment with tuning in my mind like an antenna when in higher states of meditative consciousness. The first time I tried to tune in to the global vibes, I got the distinct impression that other people out there could sense me tuning in. As Harvard University clinical psychologist Timothy Leary had recommended, I was ready to "Turn on, tune in, and drop out." Some of the psyches that I could sense were Buddhist monks, and I even thought that there might be members of the United States Military or associated with various governments paying attention, and possibly some secret societies who seemed to notice me tuning in. This instigated the inner skeptic in me, not wanting to be paranoid, and I mentally made it clear that I needed a big, tangible sign before I was going to proceed any further.

The very next morning, I walked down to the local coffee shop for a cup of joe. It was right next door to the entrance of a Tai Chi studio. Upon exiting the shop with my coffee, I noticed a pale, muscular man with long red hair standing at attention outside the entrance to the Tai Chi dojo. We made eye contact, and I unassumingly made pleasant small talk with him. Curious to learn more about Tai Chi from him after finding out that he had just come from the dojo, I invited him back to my apartment up the street at the time. As soon as we got to my house, it became clear to me that something very out of the norm was going on.

His eye contact was not like all eye contact; it was like eye knowing. Several times I got the distinct impression from his extroverted and synchronously animated gestures that he was picking up on my thoughts. The moment that I realized this, I looked over at him, and he said out loud, "Most of this happens like this," as he was gesturing back and forth between our heads with a pointed index finger. I then mentally asked him if there was any way I could help him, and he instantly said out loud, "Some of us are like gargoyles." He then showed me his United States military ID and told me he was raised by the Shaolin Temple, and we talked about Tai Chi for a little while. I felt inspired to try Tai Chi with him after having practiced my own free-form version of it for years playing hacky sack, skateboarding, snowboarding, and dancing, and it felt natural. In fact, at one point, we sparred playfully with our astral projections until my out-of-body energetic field completely eradicated his. I felt like I was being tested to an extent. I played with the Sun's energy and did a small but noticeable amount of cloud bursting for the first time that day. He was impressed, called me a Tai Chi master, and told me that one day, I would be powerful enough to affect a whole tree. I got the distinct intuitive impression that he was looking for me, and could be the sign that I was asking for.

As soon as this occurred to me, he immediately told me that "*they* have a job for me," at which point I noticed a golden glimmer in his aura, as he handed me the government insurance packet that he had received in the mail for himself that day as a sign for me. He then said that *they* would pay me even if I wanted to travel outside of the country. He then said that *they* had a ritual that was usually done by writing a number on a rice wafer, which the individual would then ceremoniously consume. We had no rice wafers at the house. I was resourceful and had Ritz crackers, however, so he handed me one of those with no number on it, and I consumed it silently. As I swallowed, the act was accompanied by one of the most fatefully ominous intuitive feelings that I have ever experienced.

Chapter Six:

The Better Than Jesus Show Extravaganza

In the following days, I had a conversation with a close friend of mine in which I stated, "If I were Jesus, I would turn the second coming into the better than Jesus show." First, I would run away, as he did. Next I would use my mind over matter when they tried to martyr me. Then I would martyr myself so gently and perfectly, in order to preserve even my enemies' potential innocence, that I actually heal back stronger like bones. And if I was that good of a guy, society should then realize it and come to my rescue. I would have a first supper instead of a last supper, which would consist of a simple glass of water. It was intended as a practical spiritual joke for several reasons, one being that I believe Jesus did one version of his best already.

Another thing that struck me as humorous about it was that it was a paradox for Jesus, by some definitions being the penultimate, who simultaneously can't get any better and is the only one who can do better than he previously did because he is omnipotent and has to be able to do anything by definition. All of that while continuously accruing a longer history of being at his best the whole time, which means his karma is always getting better in a sense. My friends started worrying about me because of this conversation and some of my other eccentric behaviors, which were magnified by the religious, spiritual, and paranormal experiences that I was having. But some of them were incredibly profound, like the time that a higher power walked me barefoot, arms outstretched, and eyes closed around a whole room full of so much broken glass on the floor that I wasn't sure that it was possible even to take one step, while my soul experienced the phenomenon amazed that I came out of it without so much as a scratch on my feet.

I attended a Bluegrass Festival in middle America shortly after on a whim, with a brand new friend that I had met on a much-needed vacation that I decided to take. Again, it would prove to be a humble setting for another series of events that would profoundly impact my spiritual progression. Right at the beginning of the festival, my wallet and cell phone went missing. I now only had the clothes I was wearing, half a pack of cigarettes, and a lighter for a three-day festival. I decided that I wanted to offer up my mind, body, heart, soul, and spirit as a gift to the collective unconscious, superconscious, God, Jesus, Allah, The Great Spirit, Buddha Nature, Brahman, collective sentience, or any higher power that could put it to good or better use. It was an act of devotional Yoga mixed with consciousness programming that I intended to apply to my whole life as a form of what I refer to as life art, and I wanted to set the most beautiful possible intention that I could. To this day I consider life art to be the highest form of art. I looked down at my hand and, for the first time in my life, could see the indigo first layer of my human energy field aura, and I swiftly created a slice through it on the fingertip of my right index finger, which I could visibly see as a gap in the layer.

I then symbolically but with pure intent ceremoniously emptied myself and tossed my soul to the wind, even offering my out of body astral projection. The next moment, I remember feeling genuinely surprised to be still there, unaffected yet, as I thought to myself, "Huh. Still Here." Then, as I glanced down at my right fingertip, I noticed a translucent white light fill the gap that I had made in the indigo first layer of my energy field. I mentally questioned, "What's that?" Something responded with the phrase in my head, "The nick of time."

Next, I decided to try to sense the universal energy field internally. The sensation was metaphorically like being at the top of a mountain that is so high that you can't see anything because you are in the clouds, while being fully conscious that you are at the peak, having climbed the whole way up and seeing just enough to recognize the sign marking the peak height. This led to the thought that since I was one with God, I too was God, to which I simultaneously, emphatically, sarcastically, and skeptically thought, "I am God?! What is that supposed to mean?! Omniscience, Omnibenevolence, and Omnipotence." I quickly decided to do a brief test of power and half-jokingly waved a finger at the ground and mentally ordered that a tree sprout up, primarily to disprove what I had just experienced.

To nobody's surprise, especially not mine, nothing happened, and I felt that I had disproved my own potential Omnipotence. Phew. Close call, ha ha ha. Though not an exhaustive test, I was satisfied that I had been as thorough as I was comfortable being with testing such a superb notion, and was quite relieved to move on. I then decided that if I were even one with God or the universe, I would want to remain hidden or invisible, so that I could stay humble and gentle, and would remain in human form even if I had other options.

Wanting next to dance with a purpose like a shaman and practicing what I referred to as my selfless trance state, I set the intention in my head to do a dance to unite world religions. I then decided that I wanted to offer myself as a spirit-controlled medium to what I vaguely refer to as my higher power, and instantly, my fingers started wiggling rapidly, my legs began to dance hypnotically, and The Force finished the movements with a wide arcing, finger pointing gesture toward the storm clouds on the edge of the near horizon. Almost instantly, a bolt of lightning came down exactly where I was pointing.

I was awestruck and broke my trance state to mockingly question if it was making me do that or just doing that wherever I pointed. I waved my finger at the clouds again experimentally with no results. Then, I wondered if I could achieve the same results with Chi. I re-entered a state of synchronicity with the higher power force such that it felt like we were both simultaneously charging up energy in my hand by converting the kinetic energy of my finger movements into electromagnetic energy, in mutual unison. When we both felt that there had sufficiently been enough charged energy, we again waved a pointed index finger at the storm clouds as we threw the ball of energy quickly toward them. Surely enough, lightning struck again, right where I was aiming.

It appeared that the cloud must have already been fairly charged up, and I suspected that the energy of my human Chi was just tipping it over the edge into a chain reaction of sorts. So next, I tried the entire process one last time, all by myself, with the same astonishingly shocking result by throwing an energy ball at the clouds. I had practiced making energy balls for a year or so previously, after being exposed to the phenomenon by my super-righteous martial artist friend Orion who had visited The Shaolin Temple as a guest of theirs, but this was the first time that I had external manifestations of evidence to validate my internal experiences. I knew this was not just in my head, too, because the crowd of dancing and listening people at the festival reacted vigorously to all three of the lightning strikes, which were far enough to be safe but close enough to be quite powerful, accompanied by the thunderous roars.

The dance continued, fueled by The Holy Spirit, and it started pouring rain. I had no shirt on, and was dancing gracefully in the rain, choreographed by The Force. I decided I wished to do an empowerment phase to the dance, because I personally had adopted the philosophy that the greatest power of all is the power to empower, and I felt like the superconscious was psychically selecting individuals around the world to empower with different gifts and abilities. Then, it positioned me upright, arms outstretched, back arched towards the heavens, and reminded all who were paying attention to the "show" of Jesus and The Trinity. At this point, my bare feet were raw from dancing on small, jagged rocks in the rain, and the dance wound to a close.

That first night, I slept in a friend of a friend's tent, but for the next two days and nights, I wandered the fields of the festival non-stop with no food, water, money, tobacco, marijuana, alcohol, or sleep. I was high on life because of the profound nature of what I was experiencing, practically drunk on consciousness. The next noteworthy occurrence for me was the following day, when I looked down again at my right hand, only to notice the first layer of my aura on my index finger had now turned to a golden light. This was only the second time in my life that I had witnessed my aura, despite having read about the human energy field and universal energy field in the book Hands of Light by Barbara Ann Brennan, which is a scientific perspective on bioenergetics, auras, and techniques. I learned from that book that psychics can see the same spectrum of light which scientists' special cameras can detect. Shortly after, I looked down again at my hand, only to see a heart chakra green hologram of a pyramid hovering just above my palm, with the Eye of Providence at the tip.

I also had Deja vu-type past-life impressions of King Tutankhamen at that time. At another time, I had a mental image of myself in a past life, hiding in a rice field with a conical Asian hat on because people were looking for me. I started to theorize about turning the Sun into an eternal, self-sustaining white hole with science and Chi. Near the end of the festival, I stepped on an exposed live wire by accident with my bare foot, but the shock didn't even phase me. I was intrigued deeply by all of this, but by the end of the festival, I was

44

running on fumes and sleep-deprived, so I started to exhibit some strange behavior. As I left the festival I made a promise to The Great Spirit to take on potential Armageddon internally as shamanic life art and devotional Yoga, and try to convert it into something positive, after neutralizing it with my Tai Chi and meditation skills.

Chapter Seven:

Welcome to the System

Going on no significant amount of sleep for nearly 72 hours straight and fasting for my fourth day in a row, I was back at a friend of a friend's house for a day or so after the festival when I felt like Satan himself was scoping me out. I asserted myself verbally, "Get Out of here, Satan!" I don't know if that was a real experience or not because even a healthy brain can exhibit psychotic features after enough sleep deprivation. Next, I tried an experiment where I took a vow of silence and was only willing to communicate non-verbally. The residents whose house I was staying at had heard my last assertion to potential Satan and called the cops because they were freaked out, and my ride had left me stranded at their house because I was not responding to him verbally. The local cops showed up and told me that I had to leave.

Without speaking, I walked back up to their front porch to retrieve my sandals because I was currently in my bare feet. When I did that, the police immediately arrested me for trespassing and put me in the back of their cruiser. They brought me to the local facility and were processing me, with my hands cuffed behind my back, in a room with several of them and my face toward a wall. I heard a voice in my head say, "They're going to rape you!" and the next thing I knew, my pants were pulled down from behind. All of a sudden, my higher power, or The Force for you Star Wars fans, possessed my legs to do a series of kick-like gestures, which came inches from the surrounding circle of officers but did not make contact with any of them. I was slightly confused by all this, and after the Holy Spirit had established a perimeter boundary, I regained control of myself and immediately dropped face down to the ground.

Then, I had an intuitive sense that they were going to hit me with some type of *energy gun*, as I referred to it in my head, and I quickly thought to invert the waveform with my Chi. I straightened out my right leg as they tried to use a Taser on the bottom of my right foot. The Holy Spirit and I, by tapping into the Universal energy field, successfully inverted the incoming electromagnetic waveform with energy such that the Taser had no total effect on me whatsoever. Noise-cancelling headphones are a common example of inverting sound waves to produce a sum total silence. The conscious sensation was paradoxically one of an extremely busy silence. The police were ironically shocked psychologically by this demonstration and locked me up in solitary confinement, after giving up on what I was later told was an attempt at a cavity search because they thought I was on drugs.

While in that cell I began to clearly see visions of myself on the walls in front of me. They seemed to be like paintings of light made with the same rainbow of colors that you find in the chakra system. The first image represented who I was as a yellow-bodied man strolling down a yellow brick road. The next imagery implied that I was like an indigo needle, Jesus was like the thread, and God was like the hand stitching up the fabric of space-time and reality. Next I saw myself as a blue Chi figure leaning casually on an indigo Chi doorframe, with a black background. It reminded me of being what I call a Peace-a-fist, which is a combination of a peaceful warrior and a pacifist, and this image also reminded me of my inner gentleman, at the same time as Ninjitsu.

The fourth vision entailed the fact that we were all analogous to parallel universes. Every soul and spirit in the cosmos existed as a microcosm that was still part of a coherent whole. My final vision consisted of an indigo chi martini glass filled with a heart chi green substance with a small red chi dot toward the bottom of the contents of the glass, all set with a black background and a translucent Chi shimmer. I affectionately associated this vision with my meaning of life because of the Y-shaped glass and the notion of love inherent in the intoxicating heart chakra green metaphor. I quite comically referred to it as my metaphysical Martini, which to me symbolically represented my own version of The Holy Grail.

Around this time, my mother had become worried about me back home after not hearing back from me for several days, and they tracked my lost cell phone and records to the Middle American state I was in. I had kept my vow of silence throughout the police processing, and hadn't started to speak until my father arrived later. My mother pleaded with the legal side of things to get the charges of trespassing and the addition of what they were calling assault dropped, instead sending me to a mental hospital to get help. The police complied and told my mother and father about the Taser not working on me, much to their disbelief. I was flown back home and brought to a nearby hospital to be evaluated.

In the beginning, I told my psychiatrists about some of my experiences with telepathy, interconnectedness, and the paranormal, which pop Western psychiatry is biased against, and surely enough, they diagnosed me as Bipolar Disorder with psychotic features and immediately said I had to start a medication regime of mood stabilizers. For the next few years, I tried every different family of mood stabilizers that they had until I ran out of options. I was frequently in and out of the hospital because I didn't like their chemical drugs, since all that I seemed to get from them was debilitating side effects.

So, I would routinely stop taking them on my own when outside the hospital, get withdrawal symptoms and have months or years of emotional baggage from being drugged to deal with, until my mother noticed that I wasn't taking them amidst my recurring existential mini-crises, and they would send me back to the hospital where they could force them on me against my will. After years went by with none of the drugs taking away the intuitive experiences that I was having, and none of the drugs effectively dealing with the underlying, as of yet undiscovered vitamin B deficiency, they changed my diagnosis to schizoaffective disorder, which is like a hybrid of bipolar disorder and schizophrenia, with a better prognosis than schizophrenia. With the change in label, diagnosis, and stigma came a change in drugs.

Now, they were suddenly obsessed with having me on antipsychotic medications, and I was not allowed to refuse. They would physically force a needle on me if I refused; trust me I did one time and found out the hard way. I tried all of the families of mind-altering antipsychotics until I ran out of options with them, too, and eventually settled on the one that I am currently on and have been on for about a decade. Early on in my experience with the mental health system, when I was involuntarily hospitalized and refusing the medications, I had to get my mother to become my legal guardian to prevent them from giving me ECT, or electro-shock therapy, against my will. She proceeded to file for Social Security Disability on my behalf, which I eventually qualified for in spite of the fact that the doctors knew that I didn't even agree with their diagnosis. In her dying days recently, she told my sister that I was the wisest person that she knew, which came as a bit of a surprise to me considering how strained our relationship became over the years because of differences in opinion. In some of her last time on earth in this incarnation, she also told my sister the the song Closer to Fine by The Indigo Girls was the song that most reminded her of me, and to this day I am brought to tears sometimes by that song resultantly.

Chapter Eight:

The Belly of the Beast:

Consciousness Crucifixion

After spending a few years back and forth between Burlington and a coastal town in Maine, where my family had relocated, I set off to Burlington again, this time intending to live out of my car and survive on my disability money. At this point in my life, I was heavily invested in my meditation practice, such that I would meditate all day long, every day, from my waking moment into my lucid dreams even, for months on end. I was regularly tapping into what Russell Brand would popularize over a decade later as the ideas of the *Mental Internet* and "Realms of unseen power." I approached the concept personally like a meditation, with some group or collective aspects and elements to it and some individuality factored in, too. I was on a mission to try to use my intuitive abilities for the greatest good, and I perceived what I referred to as group meditation as a highly efficient, incredibly intelligent way to get a lot done with minimal effort in an attempt to work smart and not just hard.

I frequently tried to convince various members of organizations that I crossed consciousness with to resolve conflicts, and tried to promote harmony in the interactions in which I engaged. As one of my heroes Gandhi once said, "Peace between countries must rest on the solid foundation of love between individuals." I was preoccupied with the rich social environment that I had access to in my internal world, and this was reflected in my more material priorities such that I was frequently misunderstood and misinterpreted as neglecting to care for myself when, in actuality, I just cared much more deeply about my spiritual priorities than my earthly ones. It didn't help that I was on the dirty hippie end of the spectrum, while my parents were both quite the opposite. I was also trying to condition my body and immune system to not be dependent on harsh chemical hygiene, while my mom, who was a bit of a neat freak, routinely judged me for my Olympic caliber immune system training.

I had chosen to take on the role of a Universal guardian angel, and was sure at this point that I was an Archangel, though I had been having oneness experiences with all of the Archangels which I was fully absorbed in. So while I had experienced a form of quantum consciousness of "being" all of them, I had yet to narrow down consciously which one I specifically was, while still just vaguely having experienced my own identity in that respect. I frequented the downtown area of Burlington on foot and regularly played music on the streets. I was under the impression that there was a running theme in the group meditations I was participating in, in which Jesus was compared to Pinocchio, The Father was being compared to Gepetto, and I was compared to Jiminy Cricket. I also, at one point, questioned mentally whether Jesus could hear the clicking sound in my inner ear that I could make occasionally. I never verbalized any of those things out loud to anyone. Sure enough though, one of the local police officers with whom I had developed a friendly relationship came up to me one day and greeted me by saying, "Jesus can hear the clicks in your ear, cricket man." I was, at that point, not even surprised to hear his seemingly random comment that, yet again, just served to prove my convictions beyond a shadow of a doubt. There were even strangers I met in the streets who called me Jesus, to which I responded, "Don't call me that."

My mother, as well-intentioned as she was, could be a worry wart, and at times I felt like she was my own personal hypochondriac. Once, she told me that she didn't know whether what I was experiencing was spiritual or if the psychiatrists were right, so she tried to air on the side of caution by trusting the doctors. I'd like to note that Psychiatrists, not Psychologists, have held the decision making authority on my mental health teams the whole way through, despite the fact that psychiatry is just one branch on the larger tree of psychological knowledge and science. It's also noteworthy to mention that psychiatry is still a soft science by nature, unlike hard sciences such as classical physics, though my doctors have historically treated their own perspectives as set in stone. All of my psychologists have thought that I make sense, despite not just thinking outside the box, but actually living outside the box. I also had a habit of going over people's heads without explaining myself, and once there was stigma people tended to assume the worst. Geniuses, shamans, and Zen Masters all have a historical precedent of being misinterpreted as crazy by ignorant outsiders, while in actuality being more advanced than their critics. Mom was concerned for me at the time, and resultantly, a social worker from my local mental health organization set out to find and interact with me one day. I later found out that he told my mother he intended to provoke me so that he could get me into a hospital setting, though I didn't find that out until years later.

He found me on the street, and I picked up on his condescending vibes immediately. We made our way to a local coffee shop, where I ordered a coffee and a slice of cheesecake. We sat down at a booth inside, and I proceeded to take an overly enthusiastic bite of my cheesecake, groaning in ecstasy, reminiscent of the scene in the movie "What About Bob?" in an attempt to mock his stigmatizing demeanor that day light-heartedly and ironically self-deprecatingly. Next, I took a fork full of my cheesecake and jokingly said, "You think I'm crazy. Would this be crazy?" I then proceeded to smear my cheesecake mockingly on my face and beard, with an overly animated smile gracing my face while making coy eye contact with him. Finished with my demonstration, I asked the cashier if I could use the restroom to wash my face. They denied me, so I bought a bottle of water and left abruptly. I walked down the street away from the shop and the "mental health" worker, rinsing my face as I went with the water.

I had made it about 100 yards when he caught up to me. Suddenly, my higher power again possessed my will and proceeded to force me to spit on his shirt. Regaining my control, I then walked to the park in the center of town to get away from him and proceeded to sit down at a fountain and smoke a cigarette.

Shortly after, a group of 5-10 uniformed officers accompanied my social worker to confront me in the park. The police all had blue latex gloves on, and one of them snapped the wrist to tighten the fit of the glove. I got the impression that they were going to use force if necessary. Immediately upon realizing this, my higher power again overcame me, much to my chagrin this time, and forced me to say authoritatively, "I'm the one who should be beating YOU up." Then, an officer said to me, "Come with me to that cruiser over there. We have some paperwork to fill out." I asked if he could bring the paperwork over here so that I could finish my cigarette.

Suddenly, he tried to pepper spray me. I ducked and avoided the spray. The officers quickly surrounded me, and with one arm restrained by a cop behind my back, I had an ominous feeling that I should shield my face by cushioning it with my left hand, placing it between the left side of my face and the bricks which my head was up against as I lay on the ground. Another officer behind me, who was so muscular that he looked like practically a caricature, then proceeded to punch me in the back of the head. No Miranda rights, no declaration of arrest, no explanation.

I then had an intuitive knowing that I had trained in martial arts in a past life and could absorb much of the force with techniques that I had learned. I braced for the following potential impact, and the officer proceeded to hit me 6 or 7 more times, occasionally yelling out, "Stop resisting!" In between blows, I would plead with the large crowd which had gathered things like "Why are you doing this?" and "Why doesn't somebody help me?" After releasing my hand from the left side of my face and placing it behind my back, they immediately handcuffed me and lifted me, carrying me to the cruiser.

I was brought to jail to await trial. The police had made up a story that claimed that I assaulted them and injured them when, in actuality, one of their own accidentally struck another officer with their nightstick while they were using it on me and injured him. There was a news crew there filming the end of the incident because it was broad daylight in the central city park, but they said that they only caught the police carrying me away. Fortunately, a friend of mine, whom I had only met once before, happened to be in the park that day to witness the whole incident. He testified for me in court about the incident, along with my mother's testimony that I would never act in the manner which the police had falsely claimed that I did. The charges were dropped, and I was admitted to a mental hospital in Vermont, where doctors determined that I had suffered a fractured rib and a concussion, in addition to the black right eye from being hit in the back of the head repeatedly with my face down on the brick walkway. That was the third concussion which I have suffered in this lifetime, and let me tell you, it wasn't charming. Ha ha ha.

Once at the hospital, I had the pleasure of meeting a man who referred to himself as the prophet Elijah from the Bible. He had written a modern-day interpretation of the current implications of the Bible, with a focus on the Book of Revelation. Eli, as we affectionately called him, asked if he could draw a portrait of me one day. I agreed, and he drew a yellow line portrait of me with big yellow horns atop my head on white paper. Beneath it was written some of the spiritual advice that I had been contributing to the group meditation yet had not verbalized out loud to anyone. Then, he affixed the drawing to a larger piece of paper, at the top of which he wrote: "Christians worship two Gods." Then he proceeded to draw a portrait next to mine of a popular musician whom I had come to the intuitive understanding was associated with the Roman God of war Mars.

There also seemed to be some confusion I had encountered meditatively about whether or not he was Jesus, too. I was under the impression that Eli thought that I was the pale green horse of the Apocalypse and that Mars was the red horseman. I also understood that Eli thought I was intimately related to the concept of The Holy Trinity, The Holy Ghost and Holy Spirit in particular, and the hierarchy of angels. I knew from history books that the battle of Armageddon had already happened in a place literally named Armageddon a long time ago. Still, the notion that the Apocalypse, or lifting of the veil, could be happening was interesting to me and seemed to be in accordance with the end of an age and dawn of a new one that was cross-culturally underway. At another point, Eli made a large chalk drawing covering a whole chalkboard that contained a recurring image from my meditations that I had never verbally discussed.

It was the see-through silhouette of a figure with a conical Asian hat on that looked identical to my mental imagery and past life memories. The complex image appeared to be an illustration of what I came to refer to as my consciousness crucifixion, with references to the concussion that I had just suffered, and humorously enough to an individualized version of the practical joke The Better Than Jesus Show, with my trip through the metaphysical desert included. I was taken aback by the profound and ominous amount of psychic information that Eli rigorously demonstrated that he was in touch with, at the very least.

I spent a lot of time and effort during this phase of my life invested in trying to establish diplomatic relations between the forces of good and evil, which I was confronted with regularly. I was trying to remind people that the battle of Armageddon had already happened and trying to establish an agreement never even to attempt such a foolish endeavor again. Once that seemed to be accepted by the different social networks, I focused on trying to establish a similar attitude toward nuclear warfare in the various political and religious circles that I encountered, from psychic spies to fundamentalist terrorists. I also tried to network efforts to establish lasting peace in the Middle East and Abrahamic Holy Land. Eventually, I decided to take a vow to be humane and try the lifestyle of a lay Zen monk.

What I mean by humane is benevolent, with all of the pros and cons, blacks and whites, gray areas, debatables, questionables, and weighing of the karmic scales. I could also relate to all of the Bodhisattva vows, and at some point, I started referring to myself jokingly as a Duddha. It was a combination of the word Buddha and the word duder (or *dudah* in my New England accent). I liked this custom description because it wasn't quite a Buddha, but more spiritual than just a duder. I also like to try to take myself as lightly as I should, and am well aware that you can't spell Duddha without dud. And I am quite intentionally relating myself to an ass. Ha ha ha. Ride me home, Jesus, lol. I also started humorously calling myself The Daily Lama. A Lama is a Tibetan Buddhist monk, or sometimes a Buddhist soul with something to offer or teach society.

I got ordained as a Dudeist Priest so that I could preside over the marriage of two friends. Dudeism is a legally valid parody religion based on the character of "The Dude" from the classic movie The Big Lebowski. He is a welfare pacifist who drinks alcohol, smokes marijuana, and does Tai Chi. I was determined to live a spiritual existence in the face of a western society which revolves around money and status, as a bit of an antihero. I even offered myself to science mentally, wondering if a triple-blind study that was blind to its own experiments would be the most rigorous scientific approach in an effort to prove the human potential.

I was trying to remain humble and small, if not even hidden or invisible to an extent, even mentally, sometimes via conscious manipulation of my subconscious, superconscious, and both my unconscious and the collective unconscious. I wanted to be as gentle and generous as possible with society, religion, and diversity while still being a uniting influence. I even resorted to Jedi mind tricks and what I jokingly referred to as a Special Olympics sport I made up, mental ninjastics, which was a combination of mental ninjitsu and mental gymnastics. I left myself mental *breadcrumbs* so that I could retrace my steps if I went far out on a mental limb. I regularly hid my identity psychically using what I refer to as code-less cryptography.

I even hid myself from myself unconsciously in Samadhi or oneness states of consciousness if necessary, coining the practical joke phrase "Your inner fool's a handy tool." At times, I also used my *crazy* stigma as camouflage to hide in the open. I was also beginning to appreciate the humility and character-building qualities of the ugly duckling, frog prince, tortoise versus the hare, scarecrow strolling the Yellow Brick Road down Alice's rabbit hole, psychedelic sheep in The Matrix of my little Glassid world I was becoming.

Chapter Nine:

What A Long,

Strange Trip It's Been:

The Lifting of a Veil

After being released eventually from the hospital and then spending one more winter in Vermont, I reluctantly resigned to go back to Maine to live with my family again, because my poverty level social security left me limited options. I had a basement apartment with room for my art supplies and music recording gear. I started my first serious attempts at recording music with my brother John, and we bonded intimately, creating recordings that eventually came out well enough to use on albums of the future. He would eventually become a key contributor to many of my albums' songs. I was playing music daily for years at this point and had already amassed a good-sized catalog of my original material. I was a regular visitor to the local beaches, often playing music for the locals and tourists for free. I frequented open mic nights in the community, and spent countless hours drinking beer, smoking herb and cigarettes, and playing music for my friends around fires. I had met a group of friends and had several romantic interests around that time, and I grew into a polyamorous inclination. Eventually, I started seeing a Psychologist who was also trained in Zen and Shamanism. This was a first for me, and I was excited to finally talk to a professional with knowledge in the fields that I was so thoroughly invested in.

We met a bunch of times over the years following, and I trusted her immensely and deeply respected her opinions. She was very knowledgeable and professional, while still being warm and accessible. I told her things that I had never previously even told anyone before, as well as many of the details that I did not trust my other mental health providers or family enough to disclose. She told me that she would not define anything in my records or our conversations as psychotic, and told my treatment team and myself that she thought that I had gifts that were being misinterpreted as symptoms. She also explained to me that I was so deep in the system that she couldn't get me out herself, but could help me make some headway.

I told her about how I was under the impression that I was Bodhidharma reincarnate, the Indian Hindu prince who was the successor to the lineage of Buddhists to pass on the teachings of The Buddha, and was the first Zen patriarch at the Shaolin Temple. I was known in that life as an ill-tempered, civilized savage and a blue-eyed, broken-toothed barbarian, but I was the father of Zen Buddhism and started the Shaolin Temple's training in martial arts, which they are world-renowned for. I let her know that I was reluctant to disclose this information publicly for fear of tainting the Buddhist culture with the effects of my stigma. I also recounted being Thales of Miletus, the Greek "father" of western philosophy and science. She didn't doubt me and advised that I seek out a specialized therapist for some Past Life Regression Therapy.

At my past life regression therapy appointment, the facilitator recognized that I was advanced enough at meditation, self-hypnosis, and trance states to conduct the session on myself with a handful of guided questions and prompts from him. I proceeded to delve into a deep state of consciousness and revealed to him that I had lived many lives before. I told him how I kept coming back to Earth in different cultures and religions around the world in order to help society, even though I had the option of going to heaven or entering Nirvana, which I sometimes did between lives. I told him that I was several famous Buddhist incarnations, as well as a Renaissance Man who was a painter and architect.

I also recounted memories of being the Sufi Mystic and Islamic poet Rumi, as well as King Tut, the young Egyptian Pharaoh. The name Tutankhamen translates as "In the living image of the God Amen," and Amen translates as "The hidden or invisible one." Next, I told him that I had been a shipbuilder from the Bible. The session was very intriguing, and I went on to investigate more thoroughly on my own in the future using what I had learned. In later sessions on my own, I realized that I was a shipbuilder as Archimedes, and a different character from the Bible than his prime suspect, who was Noah.

In subsequent years, I had vivid impressions of having been the wise man Balthazar from the Bible who gave Jesus Myrrh, the funeral incense, for the first Christmas. My friends would occasionally call me Saint Nick as a practical joke, but don't tell the kids that for everyone's sake, I beg of you.

I also remembered that I was the Taoist Priest Zang Sanfeng, who started the practice of Tai Chi at one point, and was the Eastern Mystic who guided the inventor of Ninjitsu about the basic philosophies and methodologies involved in the creation of it. In many Eastern lives I was referred to by cultural peers as what they call a Dragon. In the East, dragons symbolize nobility, wisdom, great power, good luck, strength, prosperity, they are soft-hearted, and associated with rain. When I psychically asked God what my spirit animal or name is, it was a co-creation process and we came up with the spirit iconography Electric Platinum Dragon. This book is being finalized and first published in the Chinese zodiac year of the Wood Dragon.

I have also recalled being the Zen monk Kakuan, who published a famous version of the original Taoist parable of the seven oxs, which is known now as The Ten Bulls. I have been corresponding with a representative from The Shaolin Temple via email, and he told me, "It doesn't matter who I am; it matters what I do." I have since remembered being the elephant-headed (in spirit, as a Tai Chi style) Ganesh to the Hindus, helping with new beginnings and removing obstacles, and patronizing the arts and sciences to them, known by Hindus and Buddhists for my wisdom and intellect. I am considered a primary figure to some of both psychic major religious traditions, with multiple responsibilities, abilities, and attributes.

I also remember being Apollo to the Greeks, incarnated as Socrates, Archimedes, and Thales of Miletus. As Apollo to the Greeks, I was known for my relationships with music, dance, truth, prophecy, healing, disease, the Sun, light, poetry, archery, wolves, and pythons. To the Norse pantheon I am known as the well rounded one who can perform a little of a wide variety of functions.

On a cross cultural note, my spirit totem animal to The Great Spirit, Sky Father, Earth Mother, and medicine wheel of the Native American spiritual tradition is The Sacred Wolf, as far as I can intuitively gather, which parallels my Greek iconography. I can relate to all of the medicine wheel spirit animal totems, and even to formlessness to an extent. God has told me that I am an alpha and and an omega, and animal behaviorists have found that in wolf packs the alpha travels at the back of the line, while the oldest, weakest wolves travel in the front of the line of wolves. My biggest secret has been that I use my alpha card in an omega card style, and pretend my omega card is my alpha card, in what I jokingly refer to as karmic poker. I do this in an effort for the collective to win the most, and only receive what I need. I actually function as a bit of a joker who is playing with a full deck. The last incarnation that I can remember was as the visual artist M. C. Escher. My purpose for telling the story of my soul is an effort to be a unifying voice for religions, science, cultures, and humanity that respects and appreciates pluralism, diversity, and individuality.

I have since been trained in Past Life Regression Therapy and the Akashic records, which are the psychically accessible records of the Universe. I have sorted through some of the mystical experiences and quantum states of consciousness and mind that I have experienced. Fully absorbed in a state of oneness, at times it wasn't always clear if I was just communing with many of the other angels and gods, or if I in fact was them because of the purity of my oneness states with them, so it took time to sort out which ones I actually was in a strictly personal sense. I heard a famous quote one time which states "The mystic swims in the same waters that the psychotic drowns in." I have also heard modern day Buddha Osho say that in the West the gurus are labeled psychotic, while in the East the psychotic are worshipped as gurus.

Eventually, I came to understand that I am an incarnation of the Buddhist Bodhisattva Manjushri. The name Manjushri translates as Gentle Glory, Young Prince, and Sweet Voice. I am part of a Buddhist trinity of Bodhisattvas, including the Dali Lama, who is the Bodhisattva of Compassion, along with the Bodhisattva of Power known as Vajrapani, who is also the Hindu God of the Gods Indra and the Greek God Zeus. I am known as the Bodhisattva of Wisdom, and my associated mantra, "Om Ah Ra Pa Tsa Na Dhih," is the mantra of the perfection of wisdom. They say that I have the wisdom of all the Buddhas, whereas His Holiness the Dali Lama has the compassion of all the Buddhas, and Vajrapani has the power of all the Buddhas.

Vajrapani is known as The Lord of Secrets, The Dali Lama is known as The Lord who looks in every direction, and I am known to Buddhists as The Lord of Speech. They say I am associated with a sword to cut ignorance and delusion, and that I have five different forms, including yellow, blue, red, a white peaceful form with sword laid on the ground, and a black wrathful healing form. I am what is considered to be a Dhyani Bodhisattva, and I function in some ways as a leader of the Bodhisattvas and a defender of Buddha and the Tathagata family. Dhyani translates as wisdom, meditation, or great. Tathagata means "one who has thus gone," and is an honorary title for a Buddha. A Bodhisattva is a Buddhist soul who is advanced enough to attain Nirvana but abstains and reincarnates repeatedly on Earth to help better serve on the front lines of society. Bodhisattvas are oftentimes not as austere as Buddhas and often may get their metaphorical hands dirtier than a more conservative Buddha. Many Bodhisattvas have vowed to abstain from Heaven or Nirvana until all sentient beings are saved or enlightened.

I want to make it clear at this point that I do not want to be worshipped, feared, or followed by anyone. While any love or good intentions are gratefully appreciated, my worst nightmare would be to be bigger than my britches and disproportionately factored in by society or even one individual. I am a compassionate soul in human being form, and am only one individual. I personally am not very fond of the idea of gurus and followers, I'm more of a "teach a man to fish" type of guy.

I cannot necessarily answer any or all prayers, and oftentimes networking and wisdom are the gentlest, simplest, and most efficient answers to most prayers. A lot of my work gets done subconsciously or superconsciously because the subconscious and superconscious parts of our mind are millions and billions of times more powerful, respectively. I also still rely heavily on my higher powers personally. I am continuing to grow and evolve, and my missions in life revolve around serving humanity and my fellow souls in a heartfelt, enlightened, and wise manner.

I have also come to the understanding that I was Raphael the historical Renaissance man. Renaissance means rebirth, and Raphael means God has healed, God heals, and God's healer. I now remember and understand that I am the Archangel Raphael to the Abrahamic religions. I am an angel of healing to them, and serve to guide human beings and protect them from evil. Islam knows me by the name Israfil with the same function. I am associated with green light to the monotheistic traditions, and to me that is reflected in my approach to interconnectedness, heart, and The Holy Spirit in everything.

At one point in my late twenties, I made a decision to embark on what I jokingly referred to as my "Peaceful Pro's-Test", which was a psychic peaceful protest to war in the Middle East, and involved intentionally abstaining from pleasure psychologically as a form of socially motivated fasting, similar to Gandhi's hunger strikes. I perpetuated this for years on my own, and am currently court ordered to continue the inhibition of my dopamine, so I'm praying that this book helps it to work.

This was all while I was experiencing something I came to refer to as "The Satan's Gauntlet", which entailed trying to make being good even seem cool again, amidst The Force and superconscious puppeteering me to smoke endless cigarettes, constant marijuana, and frequent daytime alcohol. I sometimes took breaks from the group meditation to take sabbaticals like a hermit, which often involved day drinking, meditating, dartboards, campfires, music, comedy and friends.

I am quite normal and salt of the earth in many ways too, and I appreciate the simple things in life as well as the complex. I have even spilled my fair share of milk, but I don't feel the need to cry about it. I'm an old soul, but young at heart, and am a well intentioned gentleman who is sometimes gruff and a little rough around the edges. I am not perfect, and in the spirit of perfectionism, I leave myself room to improve, learn, and gain wisdom from any accidents or growing pains along my soul's journey, while trying to do my best to be humane and evolving towards my highest potential. I don't know everything. Even God doesn't know what beings with free will are going to do next.

I don't mind if you suspend judgment and do not commit to believing everything that I say. In fact, I would even encourage you all to meditate on what I've presented and draw your own conclusions if you are well-informed enough to do so, and to become as knowledgeable as necessary about any unknown topics before committing to any belief. After all, the greatest power of all is the power to empower, and knowledge is power, while if you assume you make an ass out of you and me.

If you think about it, telekinesis and telepathy would be God's gentlest, most efficient, direct, and common use of force and means of communication, so it is up to all of us to use our minds wisely. Nonlocality and superpositioning in quantum mechanics, as well as quantum entanglement of the Universe make telepathy the smartest form of communication, and the influence of consciousness on the physical world has been scientifically demonstrated. That means that everyone's consciousness has access to a rich wealth of interconnectedness, and that the power of the mind should not be underestimated. The gentlest form of an Apocalypse would be a mental lifting of the veil, and gentleness is a virtue. I hope your mind is operating on a high enough level to catch everything you should.

If you raise your state of mind and consciousness to meet the level of excellence that is present in all of divinity or excellence, you may come to find yourself closer to the mind of God or Buddha Nature as well, maybe eventually communing and co-creating with the rest of divinity. The spirit of the Universe is present in everything, even the abyss or void. Christians call it the Holy Spirit or Holy Ghost. Hindus have a philosophical trinity model of their monotheistic translation called Brahman that states that God, or the Supreme Ultimate reality is everywhere, God is nowhere, and synthesis, which is relevant to everyone in a self-creating natural world. Islam has the Nation of Islam, and says that Jesus was the penultimate prophet, while the early Gnostic Christians believed deeply in fostering their own personal relationships with The Holy Spirit and God. Jews have Zion, which is more a state of soul than just a physical place to many enlightened Jews, and many Rastafarians too. Buddhists have Buddha Nature. The New Age sometimes refers to it as Christ Consciousness. Scientists have the Unified Field.

Any good divinity would share the wealth and the power in a modern evolved society, and would function as a form of democratic divinity, a conscious co-creation process. So what would God do? Maybe we should all ask ourselves that more often. Would the state of a heart and soul function as security gates and filters between the aspiring human and their own supernatural divine endowment? The monotheistic traditions assert that man was made in God's image, so how would that work? And if you don't ascribe to the notion of God, as even God wouldn't too to an extent if the power was benevolently and generously distributed, in a scientifically intelligently designed Universe like ours, nature itself would be endowed with every property necessary scientifically via quantum mechanics and cosmometry to function excellently. Excellent is the most basic and universal definition of the word divine. The supernatural, after all, is just the super parts of nature, which is actually super normal and super natural for nature to be and evolve to become.

Chapter Ten:

The Heartbeat Goes On

Over the years, I released three successful albums as a singer-songwriter and producer, hitting heights on various indie music charts internationally, with my music appearing on indie and college radio stations around the globe, and in some popular blogs and magazines with some rave reviews. My fourth album, titled Metaphysical Sherpa: Dirty Fractal Sacrament, is a companion to this book. Some of the parts of my professional recordings were even recorded in mental institutions while being incarcerated, drugged, and basically martyred. However, I like to live by the slogan, "You can't martyr me!" To me, all of my suffering is what I refer to as a traumedy, a trauma-comedy. I go by the name 'Meditative Animal' professionally in my music career, and my own production, publishing and indie record label is Moonlit Creative Works. I am an indie alternative folk rock singer songwriter with influences from jazz, blues, funk, soul, hip hop, reggae, and world music. My fourth album, being released in conjunction with this book, features Killah Priest from The Wu-Tang Clan, and another song features G. Love, who was nominated for a Grammy Award in recent years. I sent a draft of my hip hop debut Lap Dance (Behind the Poles) featuring Killah Priest, to him in an email along with an explanation of some of my past life identities, including Bodhidharma, Tutankhamen, and Manjushri, to which he responded with a two-word email that said, "Nice yo."

Amidst my various spiritual and creative pursuits, I have also been working on some philosophical ideas. In my early thirties, thanks to the encouragement of some friends, I attempted to get one of my philosophy of science papers published in a peer-reviewed philosophy journal. I was rejected by three or four of the top journals at the time. At the age of 42, I decided to try one more time to be published by a peer-reviewed journal, and with only a handful of edits from my original paper, I was reviewed and accepted for publication by The International Journal of Research and Scientific Innovation. My paper entitled Points About Points with A Point: Nature of Smallest Scale Universals is included in the journal's Volume X Issue XII as of January 5, 2024. It is a groundbreaking and revolutionary paper with some ideas relevant to almost every arena of science. I will quote one of my lyrics to give a poetic summary since it is the UniVERSE, not the UniPROSE:

"It's just like thin air, because it came from there.

Naturally strange, but not endowed to change."

The paper is included at the end of this book if you have any interest in why there is something instead of nothing, why the something that does exist is approximately empty, why the speed of light is a functional speed limit, why and how time and space could be perceived as warping in Relativity, philosophical reasoning for the uncertainty principle, and several other topics, including singularities like the Big Bang, and a recipe for a unified theory. The following is the first paragraph and introduction of the paper.

"The nature of the smallest scales theoretically possible can have large-scale ramifications when the large scale is considered as the philosophical sum of its parts. When considered cumulatively, the nature of the smallest scales can really add up to some larger scale repercussions. Even in the mystery of how something could exist instead of nothing, something existing at all is made more feasible by the realization that it is only asking the smallest possible amount, an infinitesimal amount, or a mathematically approximately equal (to zero) amount for the smallest scales to manifest as a phenomenon. This means that in one light, it's only asking for a whole lot of approximately nothing for a whole lot of stuff to manifest. That sounds approximately like more reasoning behind how something could exist at all than just not knowing. (It also parallels the predominantly empty physical world science has uncovered.) The nature of the smallest scales has other philosophical insights to offer as well. This paper aims to investigate the philosophical nature of the smallest scales, some of the small and large-scale relationships that are implicated by those philosophies, and some of the different repercussions that are results of the philosophies involved."

(The International Journal of Research and Scientific Innovation, Volume X, Issue XII, published January 5, 2024)

Throughout my life, I have continued to experience a rich tapestry of diverse "Paranormal" phenomena. I have also read the book SUPERNORMAL: Science, Yoga, and the Evidence for Extraordinary Psychic Abilities by Dean Radin, Ph.D., with a foreword by Deepak Chopra. It reveals that what is considered paranormal and parapsychology is actually scientifically a soft science, not a pseudo-science, with similar evidence correlation data to statistical significance results of other soft sciences, like psychology and sociology experiments. It also says that studies have shown that meditation can increase the amount of paranormal activity and abilities of the meditator. There is also evidence for increased paranormal activity in the demographic which includes musicians. I have been saying the word paranormal because that is the commonly accepted normal term for it, but the book's main point was that that type of phenomenon is actually quite normal. Supernormal even.

I'll impart to you a Ghost story that I experienced, which may haunt some of you more than others. I was, at one point, sitting still in deep silent meditation close to Halloween with my mother's German shepherd dog lying on the couch next to me. Suddenly, I got the distinct intuitive impression that there was a negative ghost or spirit in the room with us. I then could see with my third eye what resembled an aura of energy with a consciousness to it. Immediately, my mother's dog got up, hairs on the back of its neck raised, growling assertively while facing the energy that I was perceiving. The entity proceeded to move about 15 feet away, followed by the growling dog. This staggered movement continued all the way around my mother's circular architecture 3 or 4 more times, the dog following and growling intently each time. The entity then left the premises, and the dog went back to lying on the couch.

Lucid dreaming as been a hobby and tool of mine since middle school, and I have even been working on efforts to meditate while lucid dreaming, in an attempt to have an unbroken stream of meditative consciousness not just in my waking life, but also in my dreams. I have also had near death experiences by practicing advanced Yogic and Buddhist breath minimization techniques combined with meditative states so deep that I experienced death and reanimating myself. It was incredibly enlightening, but don't try this at home, lol, seriously. I trained for years before I was able to achieve my results, making small strides safely until I had reached my goal. It actually came in handy as good practice, because when the initial wave of Covid hit, I fell ill, and because of my COPD from smoking, at one point I had another near death experience.

My nickname amongst some of my best friends is The Claughing Duddha, because I oftentimes laugh vigorously while coughing from smoking big hits of Mary Jane. I have even lost consciousness from exacerbated coughing when I first tried dabs. One time, during my first experience with Corona virus, I was exacerbated coughing to the point where I had another near death experience. I was trying to coexist symbiotically with the virus, in an effort to tame and evolve it to a gentler version of itself that wasn't lethal and was symbiotic and functioning karmicly in accordance with The Dharma, so that it could then become the alpha virus.

I live in a modest home I call my temple with my rescue pup Fiona, and have a music studio where I self-produce and self-publish my music as my own independent record label. I play guitar, hand percussion, harmonica, and sing as my primary instruments, though I also dabble in melodica, lap steel, singing bowls, bass, keyboards, guitarlele, and Native American flute. Decades of intensive guitar playing left me with Carpal Tunnel Syndrome, so nowadays I am primarily a recording artist. I am currently also invested in furthering my education and moonlighting charitably as a complementary therapist under the name Metaphysical Sherpa.

After the passing of my mother, who always had the best intentions, I successfully petitioned to have one of my best friends become my guardian. She works in private nursing professionally, and while we have very different perspectives on some things, we get along great and mutually respect each other's varying opinions and voices. I am extremely excited to have a say in my medical treatment which represents me accurately for the first time in about two decades.

I would love to start some type of nonprofit organization that facilitates group meditations, transcendental meditators, and promotes harmony and well-being. It has been shown that group meditations can scientifically reduce crime rates significantly in cities, and that just a handful of advanced Transcendental Meditation practitioners can achieve comparable results to large group meditations. I also think that it could be a worthwhile endeavor to research scientifically turning the Sun into a self-sustaining, eternal white hole in order to avoid an otherwise predictable supernova and end of the Earthly world. That's something I'm looking into, even if it had to get done with Chi or God. Additionally, I think that a truly comprehensive Unified Theory of science may very well both need the concept of religion, and simultaneously prove the validity of it.

I thank you from the bottom of my heart for taking the time to read the tale of my journey so far, and again, encourage everyone to meditate on what I've presented and come to your own conclusions, doing further research if I have piqued your curiosity about any of the topics I've covered here. I've tried to give this story some educational value, so please follow up on any topics you're interested in to get the most out of this experience. I will conclude the autobiographical portion of this book with a stream of consciousness which I wrote as a young adult to more poetically leave you with a few of my closing thoughts. It is called Silent Suffering Symphony. I wish you all much love and many blessings. Namaste for another day!

Silent Suffering Symphony

From chaos rises order overrides interpretations of that order are our looking glass sees only Light waves crashing off Material cages can confine material minds are raised on Television dreams of getting rich by sending useless information To a use addicted nation happiness is in a pill,

But it's gonna be a short trip down a long dark road If we still think we'll find it there then We've been fooling ourselves

If we can't see there's more to us than me and greedy egoism fuels our individuality In this tight knit duality The bigger picture balances our rights and wrongs on Scales not scaled to human minds are used to judge another mind yet they don't really judge themselves,

But that's the point,

If we could see one light in every face of this life force, The light would be so bright it blinds your eyes, So they you shut and you stop seeing The physicalities of beings, The harsh realities of being, But your two eyelids can't block Unseen rays of love come pouring in past simple barriers And now you can finally see,

With your wide eyes the real world 'round you now Is full of hearts that sympathize with asymmetrical similarities of one and all of a sudden,

As you realize the direction of our humanistic drama,

You recognize the softly spoken goodness of our hearts,

As it emerges from disorder,

A silent suffering symphony,

As conducted by the chaos.

Other Perspectives

The following section consists of biographical contributions authored by various friends and family, as well as professional opinions.

Nick M. And Me

My name is Clint Ellis, I'm a father, husband, support specialist and musician. I grew up in the greater York Maine area playing in many punk, hardcore, and metal bands. Toured up and down the northeastern part of the states from Bangor Maine to Hartford Connecticut and many, many venues in-between. Music, though not as important to me now as it once was, has always been a major part of my life.

It was the summer; my friends and I had gathered at a house party. At this house party that occurred once or twice a year, there was always live music. The band I was in at the time was not playing but one of my friend's bands was. We arrived a bit early to help them set up what would be the sound system for the night and began to kick the party off. I was not aware that there would be multiple musicians at this party as it was my first time being at this house.

A few hours later the place began to fill up with people, and the music began, but to my surprise it was not a voice or song that I had ever heard before. I remember going downstairs to the basement where the voice I had never heard before, that was accompanied by an acoustic guitar, was coming from. As I turned the corner, I saw this man sitting on a stool, guitar in hand, and singing like anyone else would if they were home alone in the shower. Full volume and not a care in the world, yet much more skilled than most of us who think we know what we are doing. This man was Nick.

Over the following years Nick and I would find ourselves at all sorts of gatherings, and would bond over our love for music, life, and world views. Though our music taste was different at times, there were always a few bands in pretty much every genre, sub-genre, or sub sub-genre that we both enjoyed. Throughout the first several years of our relationship we would spend hours drinking and smoking by a fire enjoying each other's company, discussing our views on music, politics, and other things we found we have in common, like growing up in loud families.

Years later I would start a job and new career as a peer support specialist at one of the largest mental health organizations in the state. After about a couple months of working there I was approached by one of my team leads and one of the case managers I worked with about meeting up with, as they put it, "a rather eccentric and loud man." I said that I would be up to it and that people who express themselves with more volume than most is nothing I haven't been around before. So, they told me this man's name, and much to my surprise it was my friend Nick.

I told them instantly that I know Nick and have known him for years. They were a bit shocked to hear this and concerned that I would not be able to work with him. I then reassured them that intentional peer support is based on relationships and connection, and that if anything Nick and I working together would be a great fit. I then talked to Nick and pretty much told him, you are not going to believe this, but it looks like the people I now work for want me to work with you. To say we were both happy about this arrangement would be an understatement. I could not believe I was going to get paid to go and hangout with a friend, and Nick was stoked to have a person on the inside, which I found funny at first, but later would come to understand why he said this.

When I started working with Nick, I had to say I was a bit curious as to why he was with the organization I worked with. In all the years that I had known Nick I never thought that there was any type of mental health issue. However, being a consumer of mental health services myself, I could totally understand that these are things that some people don't find comfortable talking about, something that doesn't define them, or something that they do not agree with at all and believe that nothing is wrong with them to begin with. Nick is the latter.

After working with Nick for several years I have to say he is very much on to something, and because of this he helped me in my own understanding of what can be, and what others just do not choose to see and or understand. I used to think that some of my gifts were curses, such as hearing voices, visions, clairvoyance, and precognition. From working with Nick, I became much more aware of my own abilities and began to accept them. Through working with him I finally felt much more comfortable and less alone when in my own skin. Don't get me wrong, I know some things like my depression and anxiety will always be something I have to work on and be vigilant with. However, many of the things that I felt insecure and unsure about had very much become something I had a much greater grasp on from the work-based conversations I had with Nick.

I do not believe Nick is somebody who would deny that mental health is something that many people do struggle with, nor that being active in your own health and wellbeing is a bad thing. Although, at the same time from his experiences I learned that nobody should be forced into any treatment that they do not feel is beneficial to them. I got that to an extent before from dealing with years of being so numb from medication that I was unable to feel some of the most basic emotions. However, when working with Nick I could not help but feel a great deal of empathy towards the emotional suffering that he was faced with from being numb beyond what I thought would ever be medically necessary.

As of now my friend, Nick, is still in a constant battle with those who seek to "help" him. If they could get a chance to know the guy that I spent so many years hanging out with by those fires, surrounded by great

66

tunes and friends, hear him explain his perspectives of the world and our part in it, he would be able to be the guy I first heard many years ago. Singing his songs at full volume with not a care in the world.

The opinion of the friendly Nurse:

Hello,

My name is Crystalann Carter, and I am one of Nick's best friends & a local Nurse here in Maine. Having known him for a while, this is my account of the type of person Nick is from the eyes of another. A little about me before I give you my outlook. I am a private in-home nurse to the elderly & have been practicing in the medical field for over 15 years now, with a Military background growing up. With that much experience, I come with a multitude of certifications, well over 10, including the certification to define medications, pass these medications to my clients, and identify their contraindications & their purpose. So when I met Nick, I knew after maybe 15 minutes of conversation that he was severely over diagnosed & overmedicated. It hurt my heart in the worst way & he turned out to be my favorite human. I like to think of myself as a very independent & non-judgmental person. At least, I hope that's the vibe I give off. Now, let's go back to the star of the show, *The Misunderstood Mystic* himself.

Something I would love to point out is that he is extremely intuitive & I have sometimes noticed, more than once, shall you say out-of-the-ordinary situations that occurred around my dear friend. The most noticeable thing that occurs quite often is the ability he has to get inside my head. He finishes my sentences, knows me more than I think I know myself & often reads my mind, meaning before I can even ask him for something, he brings it to me, or the best one yet, I'll say, "Hey Nick, blah, blah, blah" He'll say, "You just read my mind, this is getting creepy," yet that brings a laugh to the both of us. It definitely solidifies the connection with him that I feel whenever I am in his presence. The not-so-common incidents occurred during a Thunderstorm, which our area gets rather infrequently. On more than one occasion during these storms, Nick will be making some profound statement & at that exact moment, and I am not making this up, from my visual perspective, a bolt of lightning will strike from the sky directly over his head & almost make an appearance of said bolt entering his notable brain. I mentioned this to him just moments after this happening & he just smiled & was like, "Really, That's prolific."

I couldn't agree more & it's these moments that stick out to me almost to tell me I am in the presence of someone prolific, not just the thought he is expelling. The sheer synchronicity & irony just goes to show that some things happen out of the realm of what we are led to believe. Between his telepathy & spiritual inner workings, it is enough to make me take a step back and rethink what I thought I already knew about this universe. Just having an open mind is the only school supply you will need for this semester.

I have even begun to trust him so much that I have incorporated some of his Homeopathic & Natural remedies for my clients whom I care for professionally. They are so trusting of him also that they, as well as their families, will allow me to make herbal Tinctures for them to ingest as well as use Crystals & Incense (Blessed by Nick before given or taken to any clients) for the healing purposes on a daily basis just by Nick's knowledge & recommendations. We even began to incorporate THC & CBD (that's weed for your squares, hahaha) into the remedies of my paralyzed client's routine, which she quite enjoys. These are 7-day-a-week routines that even the family has agreed to keep up with when I am not present, so much so that they have begun to make notable progress physically & pain-wise, as well as weaning off of some & dropping some other big pharma medications completely from their daily routines. Even something as small as changing the types of vitamins vs. heavier medications. Just recently, in early December 2023, a medical miracle with one of my clients occurred, to the astonishment of us all.

Her paralyzed right side is moving in the direction of the client herself, witnessed by her entire family & me. My boss was immediately notified & became so overwhelmed with pride. These improvements are being noted on a daily basis on her Insurance paperwork & within the company that I work for. Most significantly, it is important to know that these changes have occurred in just a few short months, and with them the differences we are seeing in such a short time are simply incredible. Could you imagine a full year of this routine & natural remedies, or 2 years even?! My boss even stated that this improvement in her is a *Medical Miracle* (in his terms). During this update, he then asked me not to change a thing in the routine established so we can monitor more improvements, with the hopes of her fully walking after 6 1/2 years of paralysis in her right side. He also stated to me that this is noteworthy within the community & medical field in general.

How many can say that they have put the time & research into the actual healing of a stranger? Keep in mind Nick has never met my client & with his help, we have evidence of a miraculous event within the human body. A few days after this medical miracle happened, her son, who had yet to witness his mother's movements, was called into the bedroom where, without any help from me or anyone else, she began, while lying in bed, to lift her paralyzed right leg & even curl her toes inward, which filled the room with tears. Also, to their witness, she was able to open her right hand, which typically remains in a solid fist with discoloration to her skin due to lack of circulation. With minor assistance from me, we slowly opened that hand to a straight, normal position. Noticeably, there was no pain to her, and we managed to give them a small wave.

Of course, more happy tears were seen in the eyes of the shocked family members in the room. Upon leaving that weekend's shift with my client, her son approached me in the driveway, embraced me with tears & said, "Thank you for not giving up on my Mom; I never thought I would see any improvement, let alone the chance that she may walk one day." I drove home with the most emotionally overwhelming feeling, and I called my Mom, my boss, and, of course, Nick with a full follow-up. The work we are accomplishing together is just amazing & I wouldn't change a thing or collaborator, such as Nick himself. This, in turn, makes me feel as though a much bigger difference than what I was already providing is actually & profoundly being made: "The proof is in the pudding," so to speak. This just confirms how knowledgeable & helpful Nick is to others while not receiving the same in return. That, folks, is called Compassion. Nick exudes Compassion & it shows.

Please see & hear it in these writings, even if that is the only thing you take with you from reading this. All of this is from removing Big Pharma & those in the medical field (such as Physical, Occupational, & Speech Therapists) who have said she will never walk, wave, or even speak again. Pretty much written off as a lost cause. Could you imagine people giving up on you so easily?! Well, not Nick or I. We are determined to make a change. Although, don't get me wrong, speech is our next task, but one thing at a time.

As a close friend who spends frequent days with Nick & his sweet rescue pup Fiona, I would like to think I can make an accurate account of who he is to others outside of reading his story. I can only offer my own opinion, which I know only means so much to me compared to the reader; just know I am in no way embellishing the type of soul I interact with on a daily basis. I spend more time than most with Nick on a weekly basis & have for an extended period. The interactions are hours and hours of spending time with him in all aspects, inside the home, out in public & just being himself. This is why I have always said he is overmedicated & over diagnosed, and I can see it, hear it & feel it in his presence.

I managed to spend more time with him than family & even his medical team. To say those who have spent less time with him are the ones making his medical decisions, as a Nurse, just blows my mind to no extent. Somehow, those are the ones with the biggest negative opinions of Nick. Let's just sum it up, and then I will break it down for you. I consider him to be one of the gentlest & kindest souls to be friends with & trust that in my days on this Earth, I have met some nasty folks & would NEVER consider Nick in that category. As a friend & just a human being in general, I find it so easy to talk to & get along with Nick. Growing up & still today in my 37 years, I have always managed to get along with the opposite sex & Nick is no exception. He is genuine, reminds you of things about yourself in such a positive way & always has a big heart. He is a man so willing to help others in a natural non-violent way, yet somehow he is royally screwed by the ones who are supposed to have his best interests at heart.

Before I go, can I just point out that Nick's pink-nosed puppy named Fiona deserves more than a paragraph? She deserves a book or two of her own. She is just as intuitive as her human is. We call her a pink-nosed puppy. Could you guess why?! Rudolph the red-nosed Reindeer vibes for days, but shhhhh, don't tell the kiddos. She is the type of pup that makes you feel seen & heard. I could go on and on about her for days, but like I said before, subscribe for more. She's a star to us and will be a star to all someday. Trust me on that.

It's a true shame that he has to fight & advocate more than most for his well-being. I truly hope that by you taking the time to read his story, he may one day be in complete control of his life, which is the right given to us at birth all the way up to our demise. Nick shouldn't have to compromise himself & his integrity, and NO ONE should. It's a human & civil Rights violation. When Rights are violated, it is time for someone to stand up & fight for those rights to be returned to their rightful owner. The fact that Rights of all kinds are being violated, Civil, Human, Patient, Constitutional, and Medical, in addition to his naturally endowed liberties, just blows my mind. In the USA especially, this is a recurring epidemic that should be eradicated. We are supposed to live in the *Land of the Free*. Oh, what a concept it was during the thought, but that afterthought seems to be lost on the masses of Pop Culture. We need to rectify this. That is one of the biggest hopes of getting this book into the hands of his peers, those who know him now & those he may get to know in the future.

Pssssssstttt, have you heard? I can now state that I am Nick's personal & legal Guardian. The courts have granted me Guardianship to be his voice on behalf of his medical situation. The best part about this, is Nick now has a VOICE & I do not just mean mine. I mean his as well. My promise as Guardian to him before going ahead with the court case was to consider Nick's opinion when making any considerations to his medical status or any changes that may occur now or in the near future. He has already stressed to me that knowing this alone is helping him sleep & a relief of pent up anxiety has evidentially begun to clear within him. I just hope this helps him & shows him that there is a light at the end of the tunnel.

He can see a difference being made & will have more of a say into his own life. This was not an easy task to say the least, but it was worth it. I have never been a Guardian to someone before, let alone a grown adult who is a few years older than I am now, but cheers to a new beginning. I will do my best & I only agree to this title with the best of intentions. Also, let me add that this was not a task I asked to take on, this was a request by Nick himself, out of the trust he has for my knowledge & compassion. This took me months of deliberation before even considering such a feat. I have agreed, as well as the court & the previous Guardian to me only taking on medical proxy, I will not handle finances, (in case anyone questions an ulterior motive) those will still be handled by the previous Guardian, as should be. I am only here to be the medical voice with the Medical history to back it. Officially now given the honor, I will serve as Nick's legal medical proxy. Wish us luck, I imagine it will be a bumpy road to begin with.

Let's all just think for a moment: If this were you & everyone always made your decisions for you, how would that make you feel, a *shoe on the other foot* type of concept, if you will? We all like to have control of what happens to us. Why shouldn't Nick have that right like us all? He just needs some more empathy & those who have his best interests at heart looking out for him. Not just another Big Pharma paycheck. That's another error in the flaw of our HealthCare system.

Now, before I go, (I know I've said that before, but I'm passionate about this subject) let me say this & say this loud. I am not here to judge my friend or his religious beliefs. I will state I do not practice a religion & I do not believe in organized religions. Therefore, I cannot make any judgments as to how Nick feels regarding his spiritual and religious feelings. I am not one to consider this when seeking out any type of friendship or relationship in general. So, as far as do I think Nick is a Buddhist Monk, my answer is, Does Nick believe that? If the answer is "Yes," then that is all I need to know. To each their own!

So I will leave you with this Tip, but only the Tip (as they say these days, Subscribe for further content, ha ha ha). Nick is simply an individual on this hurtling rock through space we call Earth & he is as Human as us all. Give the man a break, would you?!?!

Entered of MY OWN FREE WILL:

Crystalann Carter!

Light from the Heart of Kanad

My name is Franklin Edward Ellison, but most people call me Frankie or Frank. I am a 67-year-old Veteran of the United States Army, where I rose to the rank of Sergeant before getting out of the military on a hardship discharge. By the time I was in High School in Portsmouth, New Hampshire, I had realized that I was a gifted child. I took care of the first Israelite jets that came into the Pease Air Force base in 1972 and worked intimately with the Carter administration in subsequent years. He had a largely African American staff at a revolutionary time for that type of progress. The military was behind on their pay raise scale compared to private industry at the time, and I achieved proper compensation for them in my years of service as part of my efforts. During my service, I became aware of many paranormal phenomena that the government and military, religions and secret societies, as well as private civilians and corporations, were not only well aware of the verifiable validity of, but already putting into regular use by the 1960s. Here is my account of some of the spectacles that I have witnessed in my time here on Earth.

As a Sergeant, I worked intimately with the Joint Chiefs of Staff and The Pentagon in Washington D.C. as well as Fort Myers, so I had high-ranking Top Secret Security Clearance. I was well aware that the government, military, religions, and even secret societies had programs and directives that they advanced for the purpose of utilizing the gifts of people like Nick and myself. At the time, many of these programs were classified, but they have since been declassified. The story Nick recounted about being signed up for a *job* by the mysterious individual resonates with commonplace scenarios for that type of program.

Nick's accounts of The Holy Spirit, or The Force for your Star Wars Jedis, corroborate with the knowledge that the organizations above had back in the 1960s and 70s. The government and military, as well as secret societies, possess intimate knowledge of the power and merits of meditation and routinely implement it in their organizations. They actively promote individuals and organizations which, while they may function independently, serve society at large.

My relationship with Nick has been awesome. As in Awe, like God is awesome. As soon as we made eye contact as *strangers* for the first time in this incarnation, a bond and connection were instantly formed. As I was drinking Nick's bottle of wine on that very first day, as Jesus would do, hahaha, his spirit moved upon me overwhelmingly. I have known him for around 6 years now, and I understand him to be loving and kind. He is direct and to the point. He inspires me to reach the highest level that I can reach by giving me his understanding of knowledge and wisdom and teaching me how to apply it the right way. His story is in accordance with my behind-the-scenes knowledge about Government and Military operations, secret societies, and religion, as well as reaffirms my relationship with him. I would validate and vouch for any of his experiences.

On the topic of thunder and lightning, in a similar vein as Nick's experiences, I had an experience of my own that lit me up as much as the night skies themselves. It occurred in New Jersey one stormy night, with deep dark clouds roaring across the skies. I pointed my finger out the window up to the sky and dark clouds, and with a thunderous roar, a bolt of lightning came down right where I was pointing. This happened a total of three times in a row. Afterward, in the same house, it was sunny out with clear blue skies. I got in the car inside of the garage port, and it was raining despite there being no clouds overhead. I pulled out of the garage, and it was raining over the house despite a lack of rain clouds. Two days later, Lauree Jones, the high-ranking secret society member whose car I was using that fateful day, died. The phenomenon was a sign that she was going to pass on. The government is well aware of phenomena of this nature.

I have held a variety of positions over the years. As a professional limousine driver, I was honored to serve high-profile business executives and famous musicians, amongst others, including restaurant owners, Broadway Plays, Madison Square Garden events, and athletes. This included people like Madonna, who was very empathic and compassionate; Run DMC, who was cooler than the word cool itself; and Aerosmith, for whom I also did some security detail at Verizon Center in Manchester, New Hampshire. After working in hospitality and services, I went on to be a professional painter.

I was chosen by Muslim, Jewish, Christian, and Egyptian religious leaders after studying with them in a study group as having the name Kanad. Kanad means Kingfisher. It is a type of fish that they eat. It also means to set aside for a special purpose. I would like to say that Nick and even his now meditative rescue Husky/German Shepard dog have been set aside for a special purpose, too. I would love it if the government and private individuals and organizations of the world would actualize Nick's vision of an entity or entities that supported the efforts of group and transcendental meditators to the benefit of civilization and societies for a special purpose.

About My Friend Nick Mirisola

I am Meghann Voorhis, and I am eager to tell you about my dear friend Nick. I have known him for almost 20 years at this point. We've seen each other at both our best and our worst.

Here is just a tiny bit about me, so the reader may understand my vantage point: I am a writer, musician, artist, entrepreneur, lay-historian, lay-genealogist, lay-healer, old soul, and a lifelong student of the human condition. I'm also one who has a lot of experience in dealing with mental struggles, both from more personal situations as well as cases in caretaking. From a very young age, while not being guided to be or to believe in one religion, I pondered the idea of God and the concept of a higher force existing in the universe, beyond what we can completely understand. I remember going through a long thought-process in my head, while I lay in bed one night, at age three, where I determined to myself, with finality, that there is Something. No one taught me to, but I prayed and talked with God regularly from then on.

I could always empathize with other people, beyond reason. When I look at young people, I see who they are and their older selves, and likewise, when I meet someone older, I see the younger person inside and get the full picture. I see the real them, the person they were before they became broken from whatever it may be. I have studied and practiced Buddhism, Wicca, Native American spirituality, and Christianity, all over the course of many years. I keep parts of all theologies with me, but I am one who subscribes to the notion that God (for lack of better work in the human language) really IS too big for one religion. I mention all of this because spiritual studies are an area where I really connect with Nick, in addition to my love of philosophy, music, and artistic expression, of course.

At the time when I met Nick, I was a busy wife, mother, motel manager, Realtor, community choir member, and Sunday school teacher. My former husband, a social butterfly, had made friends with Nick and a lot of great people in town. We lived in an upscale neighborhood, but a few times a year, we would go around to our neighbors, warn them that there was going to be noise, send our children to their grandmother's house, and have huge parties, eventually inviting local and not-so-local live bands to play. I would have to say that Nick may have been one of the catalysts to inspire others to show up with their instruments.

You see, first our parties were slightly smaller, quieter, and more low-key. My husband would get everything started, and people would begin showing up. We would always have a fire going outside. At a certain point early in the night, you'd be walking through the basement out to the fire, and through the smokey mist, you'd hear these beautiful or funky/cool tunes and meaningful lyrics floating through the air, making for the nicest mood. Was the radio on? No. Hey! It's Nick! He always created an amazing vibe, just by quietly playing in the background.

Eventually we ended up having bands come to the parties, and we really loved the times when Nick agreed to take a turn in the spotlight and play for everyone on center stage, even though his goal was and is never to be "center stage." He just ends up there because has these thoughts, feelings, and ideas that really must be shared. His music is intoxicating. His heart is full; his message is clear. I believe him being there playing gave us and our friends the idea of bands coming in and playing sets, which turned into years of parties like these.

Over the years, I've come to find that Nick is as genuine, authentic, and decent a human as you can find. He's a natural born philosopher, musician, and storyteller. It's inspiring to me that he seems to be quite in tune with his life's purpose, between all the things he has already done and what he's doing now, including pursuing higher education so diligently in his areas of his interest, constantly expanding his knowledge base, fine-tuning his expertise, and working on his many creative projects. It's wonderful to see him pursuing his passions, and writing, making music, creating art, taking part in meaningful discussions, and speaking his truth. I can see him thriving.

I know it hasn't always been very easy. It's common for someone who perceives and thinks on a deeper level than most other people to be misunderstood. I've seen him work very hard. I'm elated that he is choosing to share his journey. He has incredible insight, not only from being highly intelligent and intuitive, and from his work as a scholar, but also from true life experiences. He's been through much. In my humble opinion, his wisdom also comes from being an old soul. A lot of what he has to say can help other people. He judges no one, so anyone can feel comfortable around him and hear his message.

Often when he shares insight with you, you realize it's very on par with what you know to be good and true, it really resonates, or maybe it is just what you needed to hear for that moment, and often when he's speaking, his eyes sparkle like a Laughing Buddha; you feel reassured that life is good. He's one of those people who reminds you that the universe is interconnected and that we are all a part of it. His warm encouragement always gives me hope, inspires me to be better, to not give up on my dreams; reminds me to continue to be *proudly* sensitive and weird. He reminds me to lead with love; that the pen (and at times the guitar) is mightier than the sword.

We are now in a time of great conflict in the world. It almost seems to be snowballing, the fact that so many people seem to be clashing and disconnecting from each other. There is so much unkindness. I feel like Nick is one who is part of the needed conversation going forward, about what the universe is, who we are, what we should aspire to be as a human race. I was not asked to, but I'd highly recommend, if you haven't taken the time to sit and read, "Points About Points with a Point: Nature of Smallest Scale Universals," that you give it a shot. I absolutely devoured it. It puts everything into perspective. If it's a little too heady or academic for you, take it piecemeal. This is a time for thinking and connecting. There is nothing left to do. The world can be a tumultuous place. I feel very happy to be aligned in this lifetime with the Zen Duddha, Meditative Animal, my good friend Nick.

My 7 favorite attributes about you, Nick

By a dear friend.

My 7 favorite attributes about you,
NICK

I. You are a WARM BLANKET OF CALMNESS.

II. The SPARKLE runs DEEP IN YOUR EYES.

III. Your laugh lines are CONTAGIOUS.

IV. Your "Stillness" amazes me, even when you pace.

V. Your LOVE OF ALL ♥

VI. Your chuckle, giggle and your Smirk
touches the SOUL.

VII. You have an amazing POWER AND CREATIVITY
within Your HANDS.

Much LOVE TO YOU,
"The Bag Lady"
xoxo

A Noticing Neighbor

February 22, 2024

Hello Open Minders.

My name is Tammy aka, Grammy Tammy. I am 54 and deemed legally blind. The best way to describe my vision is: I am not Stevie Wonder blind. I am looking through waxed paper. My vision is not non-existence just blurry.

The reason I am disclosing said information is directly related to my hand written submission to the book. It's hard for me to use a computer and type. Please forgive my OLD SCHOOL version.

Nick and I have been friends for a few years now. He is my neighbor two houses away in a quaint New England Town.

The dictionary describes a friend as follows...

A friend is a person whom one knows and with whom one has a personal bond of mutual affection

Nick fits that description in every fashion. We share a bond that cannot be broken by even the worlds most celebrated Tug-O-War team I have the utmost affection towards Nick which I have no doubt is reciprocated

Conversations between Nick **and** I range from Kindergarten level songs about relish. (yes the condiment) to in depth discussions about mathematical wonders such as fractal measurements. These impromptu talks both heighten and enlighten our senses physically and mentally.

2

Lets talk about TALENT! In spades
or any other term of mass quantity
you choose.
   Nick is a phenominal and unique
muscian with high accolades under
his belt. Creativity resides in the
nuclei of Nicks soul. He writes his
own, original songs. Production and
recordings are also mastered in his
in his studio.
   Nick is self taught at playing a
wide variety of instruments. There are
to many for me to jot down.
   Heart and soul are vital foundations
for Nick and I.. Upon listening to
many tracks dispersed amongst his
numerous albums, my soul soars. Imagine
a bird high on a pine tree branch. Wings
gloriously spread and flight begins.
Many songs mimick what must be that
very feeling. Imagine your soul.
   Nick also has a flair for the artistic
side of life. Nicks perspective on beauty
is beautiful in and of itself. a paper
sketch drawing hangs on his living room
wall.
   One uses PRICELESS when assigning
value to fine art. This particular sketch
IS PRICELESS!!
   Thanks to Nicks generousity said
drawing is accompanying his book.
Please take some time when viewing.
I promise you'll be a better person for it.

3

Nature seems to take on a surreal
and bewildering aspect, when Nick is
present. Trees are a vibrant green, the
sky a more brilliant blue. Rain takes
on a whispering, melodic song of it's
own. Nick instinctively and intuitively
knows every word.

Lightning !!! Oh, boy. What shall I
say about this most controversial subject?
First of all, I consider myself to be
of sound mind and body. I am a
college graduate Paralegal. Through
experience of trials and errors Street Smart.

One summer evening a few of us friends
were enjoying ourselves on Nicks back-
yard deck.

The wind started to do that magical
invisible dance it does. The electric energy
stirred up the air. A slow and deliberate
rain began to disperse tiny transluscent
drops.

It didn't take long before the clattering
sound of thunder errupted. I closed my
eyes for a brief moment. Do I dare ask?

Nick can you direct the next bolt
of lightning for me? I wish it to go away
from me and your guests. As sure as sure
can be Nick raised his hand and pointed
his index finger aiming at the sky.

The next bolt of lightning came up from the
ground right into Nicks outstretched hand.
Nick directly deflected said bolt into
the dark space. All guests safe and sound.

83

4

I'm not easily persuaded and firmly hold on to my beliefs. Nicks story is not only self validating to him, but also to me. I was and am still intrigued.

I have been diagnosed with Bipolar Manic/depressive. Many years on anti-everythings. In 2021, I slowly stopped taking my Big Pharma drugs. Big Pharma no longer has me in chains. By far the best decision I have ever made. My family and friends are welcome to form their own opinions.

Every human has mood swings. The medicines prescribed to me were supposed to help with them. Honestly I prefer my swinging moods. The side effects of said medicines were far worse than the cure.

Nick is also a long time slave to Big Pharma. He's been a pin cushion for several years now. He just wants a chance to have a say in what and how much medicine is put into HIS BODY!

I've, in all my travels, never encountered a more peaceful, compassionate, centered kind, generous 'Zen Monk. He is a cool DUDE and believes in Buddism. He refers to himself as BUDDAH. Very fitting.

For those of us whom have had the pleasure of meeting Nicholas David Mirisola, Yay for your team! For those who have not fear not. Next time you see a bolt of lightning listen carefully. Don't be afraid. It might just be Nick saying hello. Love my
Grammy
Tammy

84

Birthday Card from Nick's Godfather and Uncle Matt

Happy Birthday Nick!

I finished your autobiography. Loved it! My continual response as I read on & on and learned more & more was a jaw dropping "Wow"! I was clueless about so much about you, and yes, definitely misunderstood a lot about along the way a lot about your journey. This was so helpful.

Thank you for sharing so much of yourself in this. It helps me to understand and appreciate your journey thus far so much more deeply. What a fascinating journey it's been!

I can also more deeply understand and appreciate your varied and deep natural gifts and talents, as well as what you've been drawn to learn and explore.

I'm so proud and humble to be your uncle.

Not sure what your intention for this latest demonstration of your talents, but there's a ton of rich material in there. Many of your sentences could be expanded into paragraphs. You've got a lot more writing in you!

Love,

Uncle Matt

Fiona The Pink-Nosed Puppy

Fiona The Pink Nosed Puppy (Jingle)

[Sung to the tune of Rudolph the Red Nosed Reindeer]

Fiona, the pink-nosed puppy, had a very cold, wet nose,

And if you ever touched it, some have even said, "That's gross!"

But Fiona, the pink-nosed puppy, has one of the cleanest mouths,

And 'cause she always licks it, cleanest nose in the whole house.

Reminds me of dear Rudolph. She is modest as a mouse.

Psychical spirit guidance, she's one of the goodest girls.

Artwork

Here is a small sample of my artwork, much of which has also been used in my musical endeavors. In High school, I was one of 50 students in Massachusetts to receive a *Young at Arts* award from *The Wang Center* in Boston as part of a statewide contest. My artwork was on display that year in The Wang Center during their annual presentations of The Nutcracker. I am also currently studying Art Therapy.

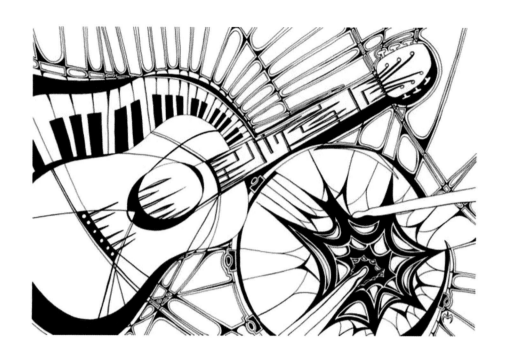

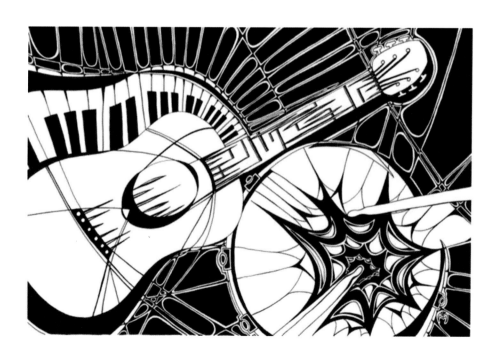

Duddha Memes

In recent years, I have been making a series of spiritually humorous memes. They feature some sayings and insights that I found to be so stupid, they're smart, or so smart that they're stupid. Some of them are examples of uncommon common sense, while others are Zen kōans intended to be meditated upon by aspiring meditators. There are even some stonerisms. I have compiled what I have done so far, quoting myself as Duddha for your enjoyment. I wanted to be sure to include a representative sample of my sense of humor in this book because it is an integral part of my personality. I like to say if there can be a Laughing Buddha, then I intend to be a Comedian Duddha. I am also currently studying Laughter Therapy in school. In the words of the great Buddha Osho, "Be a joke unto yourself."

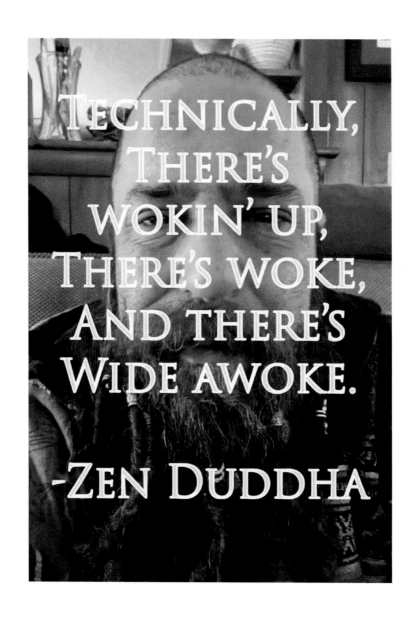

Nothingness is simple.
And nothing is simple.
Too.
-Zen Duddha

Nothing stands
In your way.

That can
Bring you to Peace,
Or
Bring you to Pieces.

-Duddha

War is
not even
the point
of war
itself.

-Dhyani
Duddha

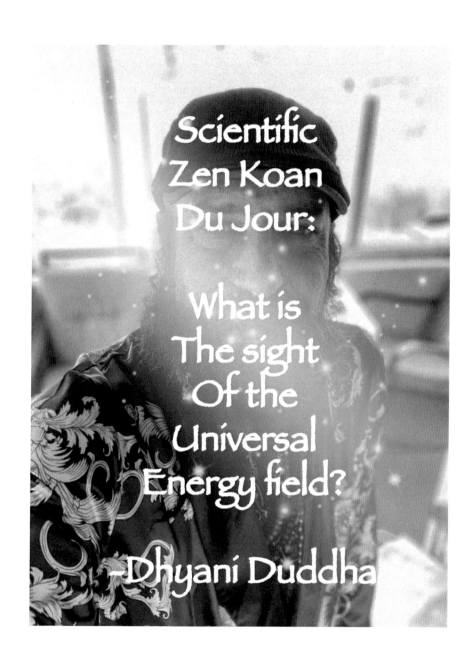

Scientific
Zen Koan
Du Jour:

What is
The sight
Of the
Universal
Energy field?

-Dhyani Duddha

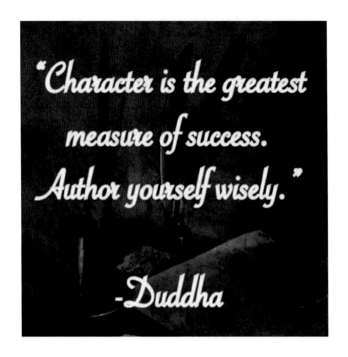

Zen Koan
Du Jour:

What is the scent
Of
Buddha Nature?

-Dhyani Duddha

We all love to win,
so win wins are
usually great.

But sometimes less
winning is better
winning.

More winning is not
always more
winning.

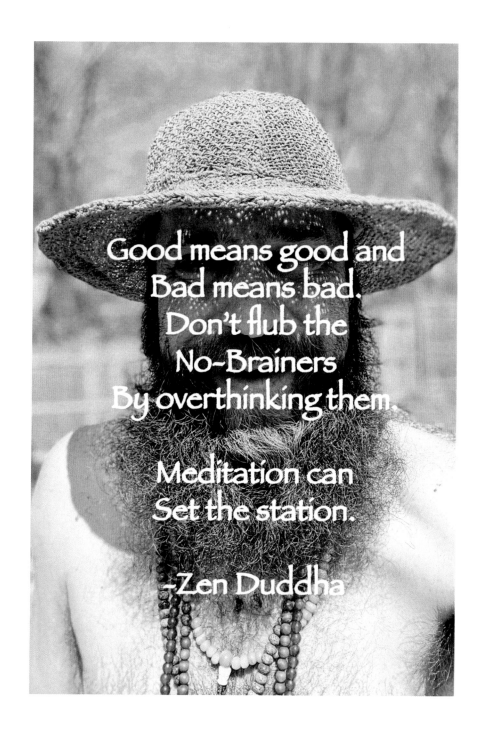

Good means good and
Bad means bad.
Don't flub the
No-Brainers
By overthinking them.

Meditation can
Set the station.

-Zen Duddha

"Being yourself
when you're
The Universe
incarnate
means not
being yourself too."

-Duddha

Silver linings
are more abundant
than golden eggs.
Mine accordingly.

-Duddha

"We are one.

To master hate:
Masturbate.

Choke your
own chicken."

-Duddha

"There's no
escaping escapism,
Unless you
Escape escapism...
Which is
Escapism escapism."

-Duddha

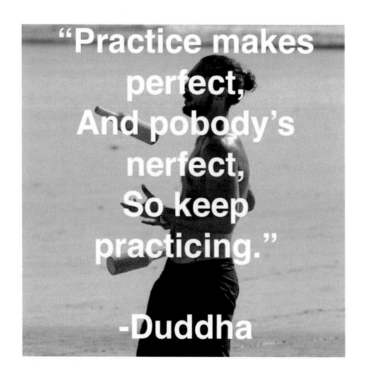

"Practice makes
perfect,
And pobody's
nerfect,
So keep
practicing."

-Duddha

Parapsychology
Zen Koan
Du Jour:

What is the
Sense of
The Universal?

-Dhyani Buddha

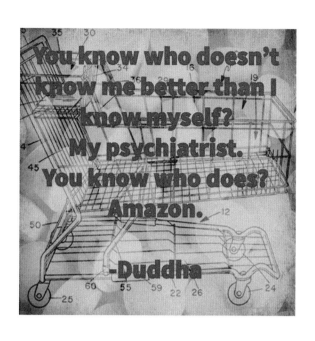

You know who doesn't
know me better than I
know myself?
My psychiatrist.
You know who does?
Amazon.

-Duddha

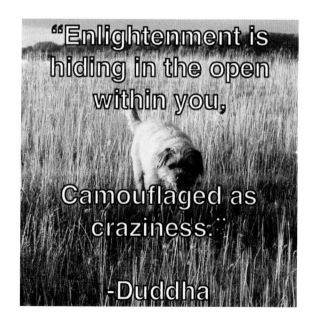

"Enlightenment is
hiding in the open
within you,

Camouflaged as
craziness."

-Duddha

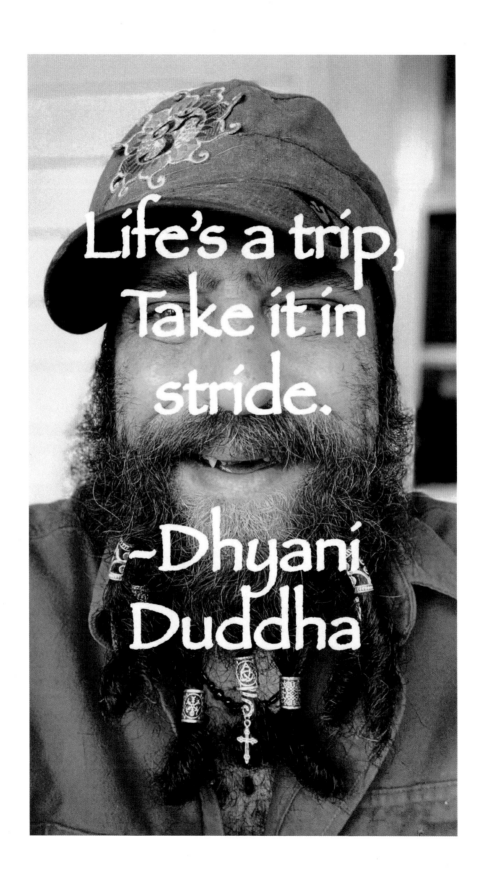

"Leave it to
Jesus
to get you to
drink wine
in the morning."

-Duddha

It's good to be good. It's gooder than
not good. And way gooder than bad.
It's the goodest.

-Duddha

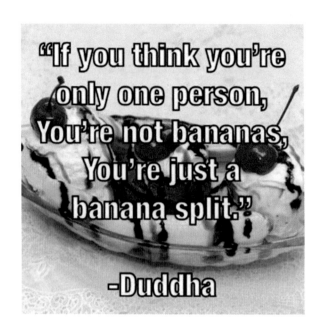

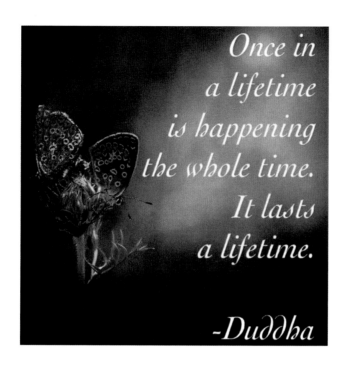

The "pathless path" leads to the "gateless gate" with the lockless lock, but you have the keyless key.

It's a codeless code.

-Duddha

Psychonaut Zen Koan Du Jour:

What is the Flavor of Savory Consciousness?

-Dhyani Duddha

My spirit
animal totem
is a
WiseAss.

−Duddha

"Emptiness is empty
of emptiness.
So it is full...
Of emptiness,
Which is empty.

Which is full?
Full of empty
emptiness."

−Duddha

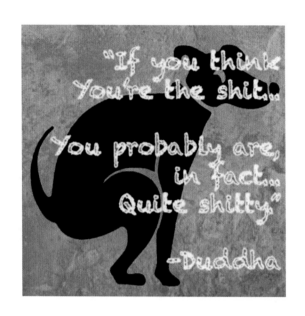

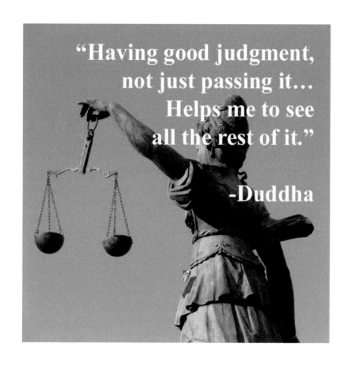

"Having good judgment,
not just passing it…
Helps me to see
all the rest of it."

-Duddha

"If you're going to practice
universal love,
sometimes that will mean
loving from a distance,
sometimes it will mean
tough love,
and sometimes it will mean
practice doesn't make
perfect."

-Duddha

"I see both sides of the coin...

And the rim job too.

I think I just coined a phrase."

-Duddha

"Wisdom would always have a heart, But love doesn't always have its head on straight."

-Duddha

"Money doesn't
Grow on trees.

It grows on herbs.

Except for checks."
—Duddha

Too much
of anything
is too much
too much
for anything.

—Duddha

127

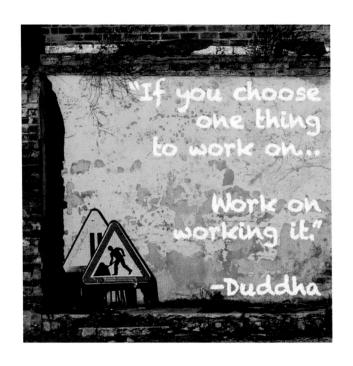

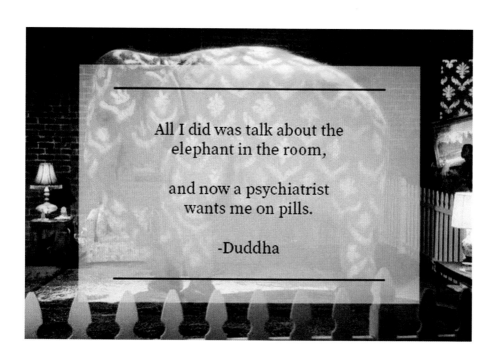

All I did was talk about the
elephant in the room,

and now a psychiatrist
wants me on pills.

-Duddha

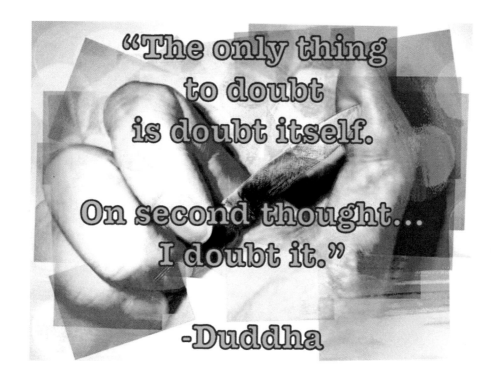

"The only thing
to doubt
is doubt itself.

On second thought...
I doubt it."

-Duddha

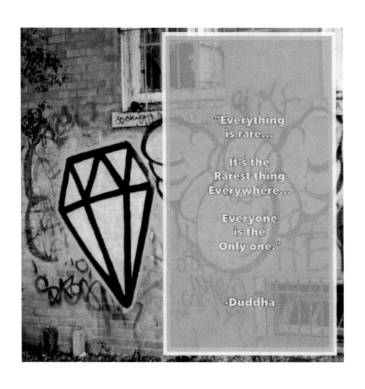

"Everything
is rare...

It's the
Rarest thing
Everywhere...

Everyone
is the
Only one."

-Duddha

"If you're going
to question
everything,

then you have
to question
questioning."

-Duddha

"Some of the weirdest stuff of all is the stuff that's not weird at all."

-Duddha

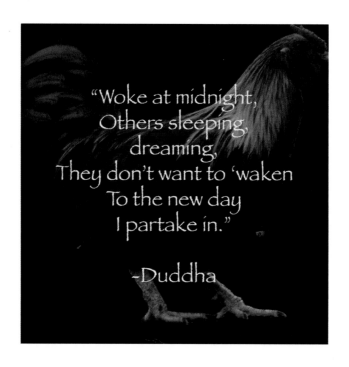

"Woke at midnight,
Others sleeping,
dreaming,
They don't want to 'waken
To the new day
I partake in."

-Duddha

JUST BE IT.

-ZEN DUDDHA

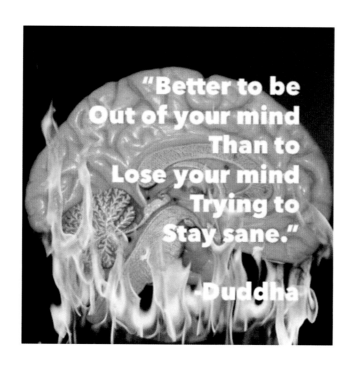

"Better to be
Out of your mind
Than to
Lose your mind
Trying to
Stay sane."

-Duddha

Zen Koan
Du Jour:

What is a
brand new
Same old,
same old?

-Dhyani Duddha

The Supernatural
is just the
Super parts
of nature.

It happens
all the time.

Naturally:
it's super
natural.

-Duddha

"If mankind was made in God's image... Then God poops. Shitty stuff."

-Duddha

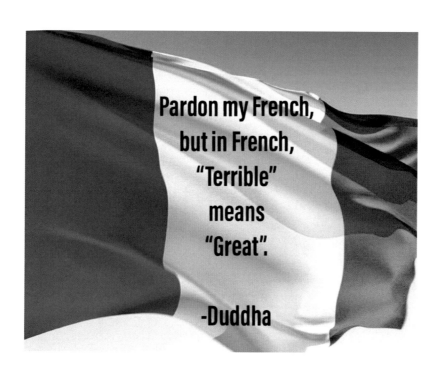

Pardon my French, but in French, "Terrible" means "Great".

-Duddha

"One way
to do things
is that there
is just
One way
to do things
the right way.

That's the
wrong way."

-Duddha

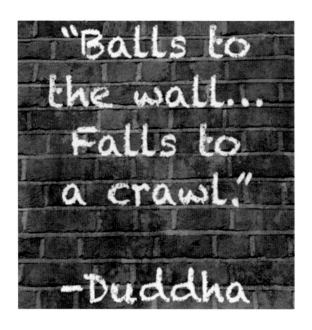

"Balls to
the wall...
Falls to
a crawl."

-Duddha

"The glass is half full, half empty, both, neither, all of that, and none of that."

-Duddha

"Some of the biggest winners Have lost everything before."

-Duddha

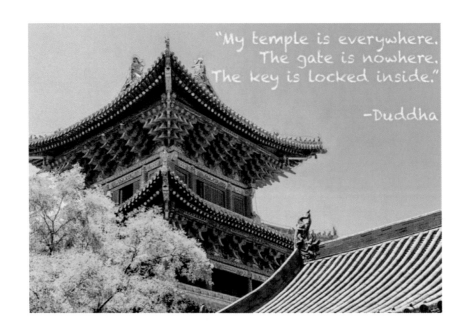

"My temple is everywhere.
The gate is nowhere.
The key is locked inside."

-Duddha

CHECK YOUR
PERSPECTIVE
BEFORE YOU
WRECK YOUR
DIRECTIVE.

-DUDDHA

"Excel at excellence. It's excellent."

-Duddha

Credentials

The following section lists my various certificates and diplomas, in addition to my Dudeist ordination, star registry name deed, and my practical joke real legal deed proving my ownership of one square foot of land in Ireland, which entitles me to legally use the title of Lord.

CENTRE OF EXCELLENCE
HEREBY CERTIFIES

Nicholas Mirisola

Has completed the necessary training and assessment to demonstrate competence and understanding within this field. The Centre of Excellence awards this certificate in recognition of the achievement.

Neuropsychology Diploma

With a:

DISTINCTION

With all rights and
privileges ensuing
there from:

20th December 2023

DATE

S. Jones

DIRECTOR

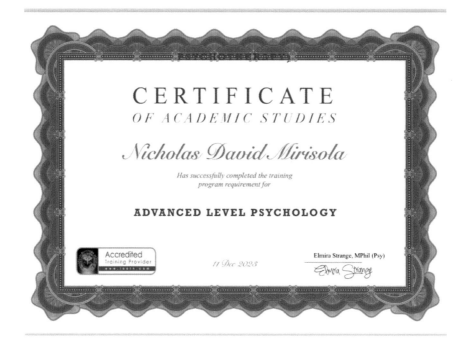

ûdemy

Certificate no: UC-9ffab957-630b-4b6a-816a-71cb33733669
Certificate url: ude.my/UC-9ffab957-630b-4b8a-816a-71cb33733669
Reference Number: 0004

CERTIFICATE OF COMPLETION

Past Life Regression - Complete Course (Beginner - Advanced)

Instructors **Chris du Toit**

Nicholas David Mirisola

Date **Dec. 9, 2023**
Length **6.5 total hours**

ûdemy

Certificate no: UC-aef8898b-4afa-496e-ab6f-28c3ab47467d
Certificate url: ude.my/UC-aef8898b-4afa-496e-ab6f-28c3ab47467d
Reference Number: 0004

CERTIFICATE OF COMPLETION

Cognitive Behavioural Therapy (CBT) Certificate

Instructors **Chris Worfolk, Holbeck College**

Nicholas David Mirisola

Date **Dec. 28, 2023**
Length **5.5 total hours**

CERTIFICATE OF COMPLETION

Fundamentals of Cosmometry

Instructors **Marshall Lefferts**

Nicholas David Mirisola

Date **Jan. 18, 2024**
Length **6 total hours**

HEALER MEDICAL CANNABIS WELLNESS ADVISOR TRAINING

CERTIFICATE OF COMPLETION

is hereby awarded to

Nicholas David Mirisola

Cannabis Core Curriculum
Dosage Protocols and Methodologies

Dustin Sulak D.O.
Course Director

Completion Date: 11/06/2023

©Healer Inc. 2022

udemy

Certificate no: UC-b834e068-8700-4943-8672-5cbf4e822aec
Certificate url: ude.my/UC-b834e068-8700-4943-8672-5cbf4e822aec
Reference Number: 0004

CERTIFICATE OF COMPLETION

Shaolin Qigong by Grand Master Shi Yanxu

Instructors **Yanxu Shi**

Nicholas David Mirisola

Date **Oct. 3, 2023**
Length **31 total mins**

udemy

Certificate no: UC-e18cfe91-1d86-4063-a7cc-2f08e9dcbf08
Certificate url: ude.my/UC-e18cfe91-1d86-4063-a7cc-2f08e9dcbf08
Reference Number: 0004

CERTIFICATE OF COMPLETION

Shaolin Qi Gong - Ba Duan Jin

Instructors **Simone Marini**

Nicholas David Mirisola

Date **Jan. 19, 2024**
Length **1 total hour**

udemy

Certificate no: UC-ca9dae36-b6f7-4e6b-9ff9-27a1b0849fba
Certificate url: ude.my/UC-ca9dae36-b6f7-4e6b-9ff9-27a1b0849fba
Reference Number: 0004

CERTIFICATE OF COMPLETION

Swimming Dragon Qigong

Instructors **Nando Raynolds**

Nicholas David Mirisola

Date **Jan. 18, 2024**
Length **1 total hour**

udemy

Certificate no: UC-c667e98c-55ce-4b91-8dab-747e4363ff7a
Certificate url: ude.my/UC-c667e98c-55ce-4b91-8dab-747e4363ff7a
Reference Number: 0004

CERTIFICATE OF COMPLETION

Secrets of Powerful, Peaceful & Beautiful Tai Chi!

Instructors **Master Gu**

Nicholas David Mirisola

Date **Dec. 7, 2023**
Length **1.5 total hours**

CERTIFICATE OF COMPLETION

Professional Certification in Akashic Records (Accredited)

Instructors **Prof. Krishna N. Sharma, Ph.D., Virtued Academy International, UniSkill Academy**

Nicholas David Mirisola

Date **Oct. 3, 2023**
Length **2 total hours**

CERTIFICATE

OF COMPLETION

THIS IS TO CERTIFY THAT

Nicholas Mirisola

HAS SUCCESSFULLY COMPLETED THE

Master Herbalist Course

1 CONTINUING EDUCATION UNIT

September 29, 2023
DATE OF COMPLETION

DIRECTOR

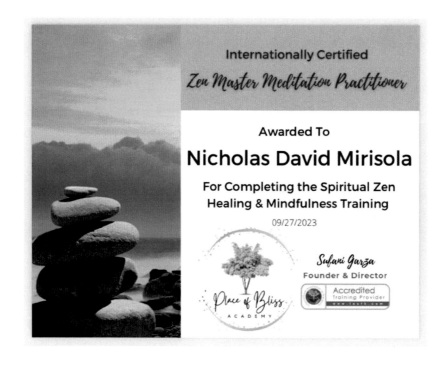

Internationally Certified

Zen Master Meditation Practitioner

Awarded To

Nicholas David Mirisola

For Completing the Spiritual Zen
Healing & Mindfulness Training

09/27/2023

Sufani Garza
Founder & Director

Accredited
Training Provider

ûdemy

CERTIFICATE OF COMPLETION

Basic Laughter Yoga certification Course

Instructors **Harish Rawat**

Nicholas David Mirisola

Date **Sept. 22, 2023**
Length **1 total hour**

Certificate no: UC-44acab6c-be23-4252-9d6c-28974fad3297
Certificate url: ude.my/UC-44acab6c-be23-4252-9d6c-28974fad3297
Reference Number: 0004

CERTIFICATE OF COMPLETION

NLP Humour Therapy To Relieve Stress And Anxiety Quickly

Instructors **Pradeep Aggarwal**

Nicholas David Mirisola

Date **Sept. 22, 2023**
Length **37 total mins**

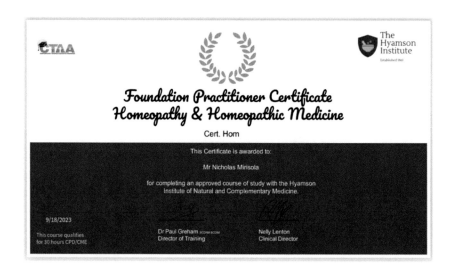

Certificate of Completion

This is to certify that

Nicholas Mirisola

has successfully completed the CTAA accredited course of

Quantum Healing

'Quantum Healing for all' and has obtained the necessary knowledge
to facilitate Quantum Healing Sessions.

Patricia Grootjans
Instructor

September 16, 2023

Date

Certificate no: UC-70739f1e-0556-401a-9583-90e73c5ce14f
Certificate url: ude.my/UC-70739f1e-0556-401a-9583-90e73c5ce14f
Reference Number: 0004

CERTIFICATE OF COMPLETION

What is Consciousness? - Spirituality meets Quantum Physics

Instructors **Peter Torok**

Nicholas David Mirisola

Date **Aug. 10, 2023**
Length **2 total hours**

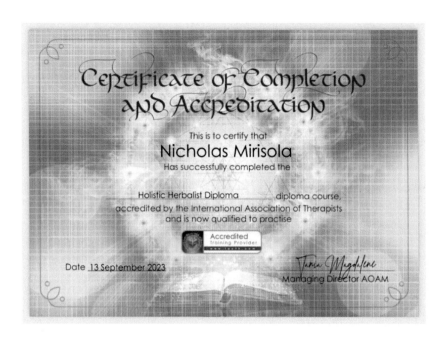

Certificate of Completion and Accreditation

This is to certify that

Nicholas Mirisola

Has successfully completed the

Holistic Herbalist Diploma   diploma course,
accredited by the International Association of Therapists
and is now qualified to practise

Accredited Training Provider

Date 13 September 2023

Managing Director AOAM

The Hyamson Institute

Certificate of Natural Medicine

Cert. NatMed

This award is given to:

Mr Nicholas Mirisola

for completing an approved course of study with the Hyamson
Institute of Natural and Complementary Medicine.

9/2/2023

Dr Paul Greham
Director of Training

Nelly Lenton
Clinical Director

udemy

Certificate no: UC-a20bef6c-5930-44e7-bb46-61728792f5ca
Certificate url: ude.my/UC-a20bef6c-5930-44e7-bb46-61728792f5ca
Reference Number: 0004

CERTIFICATE OF COMPLETION

Certification in Crystal Healing - Accredited Masterclass

Instructors **Prof. Krishna N. Sharma, Ph.D., Virtued Academy International, UniSkill Academy**

Nicholas David Mirisola

Date **Dec. 29, 2023**
Length **2.5 total hours**

udemy

Certificate no: UC-17833e71-ed8b-47bc-93f2-9a2b266da775
Certificate url: ude.my/UC-17833e71-ed8b-47bc-93f2-9a2b266da775
Reference Number: 0004

CERTIFICATE OF COMPLETION

Power of the Mind in Health and Healing

Instructors **Keith R. Holden, M.D.**

Nicholas David Mirisola

Date **Nov. 3, 2023**
Length **5.5 total hours**

udemy

Certificate no: UC-55021393-c2bc-4d56-988e-f5b88e3b2471
Certificate url: ude.my/UC-55021393-c2bc-4d56-988e-f5b88e3b2471
Reference Number: 0004

CERTIFICATE OF COMPLETION

Diploma in Music Therapy - in an hour (+14 hours study!)

Instructors **Chris Sivewright, Brandon Hoadley**

Nicholas David Mirisola

Date **Aug. 27, 2023**
Length **1 total hour**

udemy

Certificate no: UC-74ef784e-7242-4b1c-bf30-fe9adac37496
Certificate url: ude.my/UC-74ef784e-7242-4b1c-bf30-fe9adac37496
Reference Number: 0004

CERTIFICATE OF COMPLETION

[Accredited] Existential Psychotherapy for Counseling

Instructors **Aman Varma Psychologist**

Nicholas David Mirisola

Date **Aug. 21, 2023**
Length **1.5 total hours**

ûdemy

Certificate no: UC-e48226fe-a5fc-4d26-9a5d-293504290327
Certificate url: ude.my/UC-e48226fe-a5fc-4d26-9a5d-293504290327
Reference Number: 0004

CERTIFICATE OF COMPLETION

The Science of Reiki

Instructors **Jessica Irey**

Nicholas David Mirisola

Date **Dec. 19, 2023**
Length **1 total hour**

ûdemy

Certificate no: UC-5cfccaa1-44bc-4bb9-bb0a-2b0b6815458a
Certificate url: ude.my/UC-5cfccaa1-44bc-4bb9-bb0a-2b0b6815458a
Reference Number: 0004

CERTIFICATE OF COMPLETION

Certified Egyptian Sekhem-Seichim Reiki Master / Teacher

Instructors **Prof. Krishna N. Sharma, Ph.D., Virtued Academy International, UniSkill Academy**

Nicholas David Mirisola

Date **Dec. 17, 2023**
Length **2 total hours**

CERTIFICATE OF COMPLETION

Occultism Level 1: Explore Hidden Knowledge

Instructors **Gilad James, PhD**

Nicholas David Mirisola

Date **Nov. 11, 2023**
Length **1 total hour**

CERTIFICATE OF COMPLETION

Occultism Level 2: Science of the Paranormal

Instructors **Gilad James, PhD**

Nicholas David Mirisola

Date **Dec. 4, 2023**
Length **3 total hours**

Certificate no: UC-9c76782d-9c08-4a08-aca3-dbd05bb26010
Certificate url: ude.my/UC-9c76782d-9c08-4a08-aca3-dbd05bb26013
Reference Number: 0004

CERTIFICATE OF COMPLETION

Nonlinear Systems & Chaos: An Introduction

Instructors **Systems Innovation**

Nicholas David Mirisola

Date **Dec. 5, 2023**
Length **1.5 total hours**

Certificate no: UC-7a2fc688-7921-4dc1-ac83-dbe36addca82
Certificate url: ude.my/UC-7a2fc688-7921-4dc1-ac83-dbe36addca82
Reference Number: 0004

CERTIFICATE OF COMPLETION

The Quantum Mind: Powerful Concepts in Personal Development

Instructors **Samar Habib**

Nicholas David Mirisola

Date **Nov. 3, 2023**
Length **4.5 total hours**

CERTIFICATE OF COURSE COMPLETION

Course accredited by Complementary Therapists Accredited Association

THIS CERTIFICATE IS GIVEN TO

Nicholas David Mirisola

for successfully completing the course
**Sound Therapy & Sound Healing
Accredited Practitioner Course**

Awarded on 17th january 2024

Tom Llewellyn, Course Tutor & Director
Soulremember Retreats

www.soulremember.com

SOUNDWAVE HEALING THERAPY CERTIFICATE

OF ACHIEVEMENT

THIS CERTIFICATE IS PROUDLY PRESENTED TO :

Nicholas David Mirisola

Congratulations on completing
the accredited Soundwave Healing Therapy Course for
5 CPD credits

Gabriel
Course Instructor
Gabriel Castillo
9/19/2023

CPD

ACCREDITED PROVIDER
#780112

verify @ https://theppdregister.com

CERTIFICATE OF COMPLETION

Sound Therapy Full Certification Course

Instructors   **Otto K. Schwarz**

Nicholas David Mirisola

Date   **Aug. 25, 2023**
Length   **2.5 total hours**

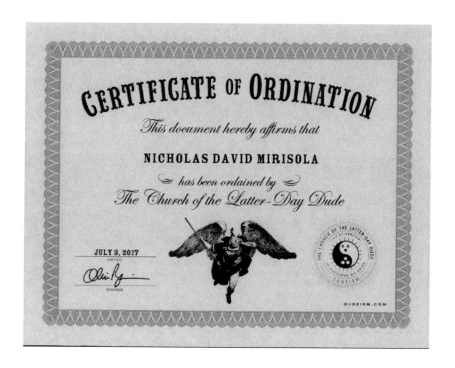

Diploma

Of Professional Study

This certifies that

Nicholas David Mirisola

*has successfully completed the training
program requirement for*

Fully Accredited Professional
Parapsychology Diploma Course

DR. KAREN E WELLS

Karen E Wells - Instructor

22nd August 2023

The KEW TRAINING ACADEMY - Accredited by CTAA - Complementary Therapists Accreditation Association

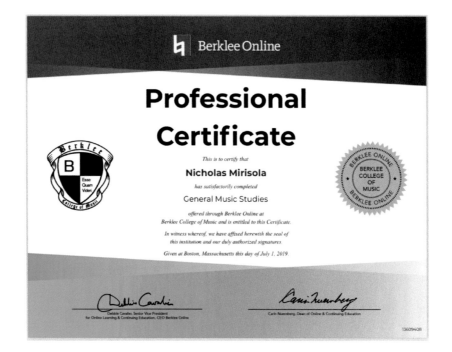

Berklee Online

Professional

Certificate

This is to certify that

Nicholas Mirisola

has satisfactorily completed

General Music Studies

*offered through Berklee Online at
Berklee College of Music and is entitled to this Certificate.*

*In witness whereof, we have affixed herewith the seal of
this institution and our duly authorized signatures.*

Given at Boston, Massachusetts this day of July 1, 2019.

Debbie Cavalier, Senior Vice President
for Online Learning & Continuing Education, CEO Berklee Online

Carin Nuernberg, Dean of Online & Continuing Education

13609408

Extra Bright Star Name Deed

Be it known to all that this star, designated in the scientifically renowned Star-Name-Registry© as:

6470268 - Draco

Residing in the boundaries of the above constellation is hereby named:

The Star of Duddha - 26th November 2021

The star's astronomically verified position is:

Right ascension 18h 18m 32.29s

Declination 62° 7' 49.08"

Magnitude 9.8990000

The public record is listed in the Star-Name-Registry© and is copyrighted with the British government. A duplicate of the star name deed is maintained in a secure location.

Dedicated to the Universe. Best wishes and many blessings for all. Much love from Duddha Nick Mirisola. Victory of the people!

LORD OF ARDMORE

CERTIFICATE OF SALE AND DISPOSITION

This contract of sale, in respect of Slievekirk Wood, Ardmore, forming part of the Lands and Estates of Ardmore and Slievekirk, (BT47 3TQ) is made on the 27th day of January in the year 2021 between Celtic Titles, a division of Highland Titles OU and

Lord Nicholas David Mirisola

(hereinafter called "THE LORD"), c/o Celtic Titles, PO Box 7093, Kewbridge, PH12 4Bd, UK.

Whereas Celtic Titles has set out part of the estate known as SLIEVEKIRK WOOD, ARDMORE, IRELAND as a scheme of souvenir plots and has caused a common form of conveyance to be prepared.

Celtic Titles has agreed with THE LORD for the sale of one square foot of Slievekirk Wood, Ardmore which for the purpose of identification is plot number S1404, and is precisely defined as a plot one foot by one foot with the south west corner of the said plot resting on the Ordnance Survey Reference point 065229900 572599200 and is hereinafter referred to as "THE PLOT".

THE PLOT forms part of the estate identified as ALL and WHOLE the plot of ground and being the subjects more particularly described in and recorded in the Northern Ireland Land Registry and forming part of the Lands and Estates of Slievekirk Wood, Ardmore.

NOW THIS DEED WITNESSETH as follows: -

Celtic Titles, in CONSIDERATION of all sums due and paid to us by THE LORD of which we acknowledge receipt and discharge him HAVE SOLD and DO HEREBY DISPONE to and in favour of THE LORD and to his executors and assignees all and whole THE PLOT but without rights of vehicular access hereto over the larger subjects, reserving those rights of vehicular access to Celtic Titles and its successors in title of the larger subjects and all others authorised by it; WITH ENTRY as at the below date. This deed shall be governed by the Law of NORTHERN IRELAND.

THE LORD hereby covenants with Celtic Titles that THE LORD and successors in title shall not sell the plot number S1404 except as a whole, specifically not in such a way that it could be registered or owned in separate titles or in separate ownerships.

In witness whereof Celtic Titles has affixed its common seal at the place and on the date of signatures below.

Director 27 January 2021

Secretary 2" January 2021

Astrological Birth Chart

Whether or not you believe in astrology, after having read my biography, you would be amazed at the accuracy of my astrological birth chart. I have read several different interpretations of my birth chart from multiple sources, and they have all been astonishingly accurate. It could even be enough to turn a skeptic into a believer. You can enter my name, Nicholas David Mirisola, place of birth as Exeter, New Hampshire, date of birth as November 26, 1981, and time of birth 6:40 PM into any birth chart generator to get your version. One of the specific natal chart reports that particularly impressed me can be found for free by entering the information that I provided on the website: https://www.ChaosAstrologer.com

Here is a screenshot of one section from my Chaos Astrologer birth chart interpretation. (Here's your SIGN!!!)

Mercury in Scorpio

The original Sherlock Holmes, you are able to ferret out information and all kinds of secrets. You are research-oriented and security minded. A shrewd and penetrating mind, you have great psychological instincts and are able to get at the causes beneath the surface of life.

Mercury Conjunct Uranus

You do a lot to fulfill the popular stereotype of the "genius," so obviously brilliant are some of the things you think and say. You have such an outpouring of insights that having a conversation with you can be a real experience. Your mind works like lightning. Words and thoughts sort of shoot out, illuminating whatever subject is at hand. You really do have very different ideas and ways of expressing them. There may also be a sustained interest in communication, computers, electronics, and all that is electrical.

AA   🔒 chaosastrologer.com   ↻

References

My music can be found on all of the major streaming platforms under the name Meditative Animal.

My website is:

MeditativeAnimal.com

My philosophy of science paper, Points About Points with A Point: Nature of Smallest Scale Universals, can be found in Volume X Issue XII of The International Journal of Research and Scientific Innovation as its original December 2023 publication.

International Journal of Research and Scientific Innovation (IJRSI)

Meditative Animal Lyrics:

Philosophical Gear

Echoes Left in My Head

(Verse 1)

I can see you connectin' with me, and a chill runs down my spine.

With this language, our thoughts can be free,

And then meet back up in time,

With this music, we feel it sublimely, and it sorta blows my mind.

Yeah, with this language, our thoughts can be free,

And then meet back up in time,

And then meet back up in time.

(Chorus 1)

It's been a long time comin', it'll be a longer time ahead,

A whole lot of strummin', without a whole lot of bread.

Sure has been a whole lot of strummin', without a whole lot of bread.

So we're just gonna keep on dancin' with that music in our heads.

Yeah, we're gonna keep on dancin' with that music in our heads.

(Verse 2)

Sweet vibrations that coarse through the air,

it's no wonder my heart plays like a snare.

Echoes left in my head from a good song

leave me tappin' my toes all day long.

If I ever met an alien, I'd hope that they knew how to sing,

'Cuz echoes left in my head from a good song

leave me tappin' my toes all the day long.

All the day, all the day, all the day long.

All the day, all the day, all the day long.

(Chorus 2)

It's been a long time comin', it'll be a longer time ahead,

Whole lot of strummin', without a whole lot of bread.

A whole lot of strummin', without a whole lot of bread.

So we're just gonna keep on dancin' with that music in our heads.

Yeah, we're gonna keep on dancin' with that music in our heads.

It's been a long time comin', it'll be a longer time ahead,

Whole lot of strummin', without a whole lot of bread.

Sure has been a whole lot of strumming,

heart and soul food for our heads.

So we're just gonna keep on dancin' with that music in our heads.
Yeah, we're gonna keep on dancin' with that music in our heads.

Telescope Eyes (Reprise)

(Verse 1)

Is it me, or are things a little stranger than they seem?
Could it be that the truth creeps a little mystically to me?
There's viewpoints here, and some more are over there,
Is it really clear, or are they just believin' what is near?
Yeah, is it me, or are things a little stranger than they seem?
Could it be that the truth creeps a little cryptically to me?
There's viewpoints here, and some more are over there,
Is it really clear, or are they just believin' out of fear?
Could it be that the truth creeps mystically to me?
Could it be that the truth creeps mystically to me?

(Bridge 1)

There's space for faith, and it's always the time for the truth.
So, I've got to rely on my logic and the burdens of the proof.
I synthesize it, I realize it:

(Chorus 1)

The stars shine distant through my telescope eyes,
At least the stars they shine though distant through my telescope eyes.
The stars shinin' vibrant through my telescope eyes,
At least the stars they shine so vibrant through my so very telescopic eyes.

(Verse 2)

One plus one always comes out lookin' just like two,
But stories of God and man can barely seem to do the same.
But there's got to be somethin' to explain this holiness,
'Cuz I can see we got hearts that'll bring us down on our knees,
I can see we got hearts that'll bring right 'round on our knees,
I can see we got hearts that'll bring us right up from our knees.

(Bridge 2)

There's space for faith, but it's always the time for the truth.

167

So, I've got to rely on my logic and the burdens of the proof.

I synthesize it, I realize it:

(Chorus 2)

The stars shine distant through my telescope eyes,

At least the stars they shine though distant through my telescope eyes.

The stars shinin' vibrant through my telescope eyes,

At least the stars they shine so vibrant through my so very telescopic eyes.

The Whistler in the Mill

(Verse 1)

I've got a delicate balance to preserve,

I found a shard of inspiration on a sill.

A bit of mental occupation to observe,

But no degree of self-diversion cures the ill.

Hibernating implications stain my hand,

So sweetly reel me in,

Send me to those gloomy, gloomy memories of the hill,

Where younger ears can hear the whistler in the mill.

(Chorus 1)

I can hear the whistler in the mill,

His smothered cheer, just a breath confined to fill

His heeded fears, well, they ran right through the hills.

I shed a tear for the whistler in the mill,

For the whistler, the whistler in the mill,

For the whistler, the whistler in the mill.

(Verse 2)

He used to dream of what he'd really love to be,

'Til he wrapped himself on up in supposed to be,

Now he's wound up in a dreary have to be,

Instead of flyin' with his spirit free.

What did the whistler think he ever had to lose?

But words like what if, could, and who knows, maybe I?

What did the whistler think he ever had to prove?
To all the straight-laced looks in stranger's eyes?

(Chorus 2)

I can hear the whistler in the mill,
His smothered cheer, just a breath confined to fill
His heeded fears, well, they ran right through the hills.
He shed a tear, oh the whistler in the mill,
For the whistler, the whistler in the mill,
For the whistler, the whistler in the mill.

(Verse 3)

I found a speck of inspiration on a curb,
I picked it up and gave thought to what it deserved.
Just enough of my attention and my herb,
'Til I could start to see the point begin to curve.
I won't let convention take my hand,
And so safely break me in.
I can hear him whistlin' in the valley down below,
Weary warnings of the whistler in the mill.

(Chorus 3)

I can hear the whistler in the mill,
His smothered cheer, just a breath confined to fill
His heeded fears, well, they ran right through the hills.
I shed my fears for the whistler in the mill,
For the whistler, the whistler in the mill,
For the whistler, the whistler in the mill.

Timed Temperance

(Verse 1)

Been through hell with love inside,

Can't say that I just enjoyed the ride.

After the flames subside,

It'll have toughened up my hide.

And by the end of the night,

can't say I didn't shed a little light.

Yeah by the end of the night,

can't say I didn't shed a little light.

(Chorus 1)

I'm hangin' in there,

maybe not up on top,

maybe not by a lot,

but I'm not gonna stop, no,

I'm not lettin' go.

What may come might toss me around,

It might make me the clown,

but it can't keep me down,

I'm not lettin' go.

I'm not lettin', no I'm not lettin', no I'm not lettin' go.

(Verse 2)

Spent all day up in the skies,

Up where the winged ones fly.

Braced my temperance for the worst,

Fell face-first, hit the ground, and I cursed.

The ground left a bad taste in my mouth,

'Cuz I thought by now, I'd have it figured out.

Yeah, the ground left a bad taste in my mouth,

'Cuz I thought by now, I'd have it figured out.

(Chorus 2)

I'm hangin' in there,

maybe not up on top,

maybe not by a lot,

but I'm not gonna stop, no,

I'm not lettin' go.

What may come might toss me around,

It might make me the clown,

but it can't keep me down,

I'm not lettin' go.

I'm not lettin', no I'm not lettin', no I'm not lettin' go.

Young and Old

(Verse 1)

Religion tells ya not to gamble, but faith is one big bet.

it's like your money ain't worth the risk, but your mind is yet

So philosophy's my best friend, with a question mark

or, could be my worst enemy, in quotation marks.

'Cuz every time I shine my little light,

the abyss can't help but seem darker,

but every little shadow of a doubt is another reminder

that no matter how I've got it figured out,

the light could be right behind me.

(Chorus 1)

"How did we get here?" Asked the little boy

"How you gettin' where you wanna be?" Asked the wrinkled soul

"Lord, why am I here?" The boy asked of his unknown God

But "Why am I here?" The old man asked of his heart

"What happens when we die?" The little boy said to the sky

"How you livin' now?" The old man replied and sighed

"How you livin' now?" The old man replied and cried

"How you livin' now?" The old man replied and sighed

The old man replied and sighed

The old man replied, "Inside."

(Verse 2)

I've spent so much time wonderin' 'bout things I can't know,

all this time, ponderin' with nothin' to show

except for the fact that sometimes it's best to question and roll

except for the fact that sometimes it's best to question and roll

'Cuz every time I shine my little light,

the abyss can't help but seem darker,

but every little shadow of a doubt is another reminder

that no matter how I've got it figured out,

the light could be right behind me.

but every time the moon comes 'round the bend is another reminder

that no matter how I've got it figured out,

the light could be right behind me.

(Chorus 2)

"How did we get here?" Asked the little boy

"How you gettin' where you wanna be?" Asked the wrinkled soul

"Lord, why am I here?" The boy asked of his unknown God

But "Why am I here?" The old man asked of his heart

"What happens when we die?" The little boy said to the sky

but "How you livin' now?" The old man replied and sighed

"How you livin' now?" The old man replied and cried

"How you livin' now?" The old man replied and sighed

Clouded

(Verse 1)

Lookin' for answers, not question marks

Findin' myself by the fire, lookin' for the sparks.

In the heat of my pursuit, the minutia turns cold blue.

It's such a seedless fruit, but it's like no one even knew.

And Philosophy burns sweetly, and philosophy burns sweetly.

(Chorus 1)

Sometimes life's like a hurricane, other times like a gentle rain,

But we can't see the difference if we're clouded by indifference.

Sometimes, thoughts lead to barren zones,

other times, we should just call 'em homes,

But we can't steer the difference if we're clouded by indifference.

(Verse 2)

Big things on my mind. I watch the little ones turn to slime.

Misfocusin' again, well, at least it's not a sin.

From God to Gandhi, big concepts crowd me,

Like mental candy, but in their wake, the

Monotony lies indifferently,

Irrelevance lies indifferently.

(Chorus 2)

Sometimes life's like a hurricane, other times like a gentle rain,

But we can't see the difference if we're clouded by indifference.

Sometimes, thoughts lead to barren zones.

Other times, we should just call 'em homes,

But we can't steer the difference if we're clouded by the difference.

Sometimes life's like a hurricane, other times like a gentle rain,

But we can't see the difference if we're clouded by the difference.

Sometimes, thoughts lead to barren zones.

Other times, we should just call 'em homes,

But we can't steer the difference if we're clouded by the difference.

Simple Adjustments

(Verse 1)

With mountains of things to decide,

Not knowin' which way to ride,

It doesn't come easy, I say,

If everything gets in the way.

Hopin' there's nothin' they missed,

Out there in that great abyss.

(Chorus 1)

Simple adjustments were all that it took.

Page by page, my friends, they're all just simple books.

So simple adjustments were all that it took,

Simple adjustments, no matter how it looked.

Simple adjustments were all that it took.

Simple adjustments, simple.

(Verse 2)

Reality's testin' my time,

Formality's bustin' my rhymes.

Adaptin' should not be this slow,

It's not when we go for the flow.

The pressure's on, and I'm tired,

Hopin' to get this rewired.

(Chorus 2)

Simple adjustments were all that it took.

Page by page my friends, they're all just simple books.

So simple adjustments were all that it took,

Simple adjustments, no matter how it looked.

Simple adjustments were all that it took.

Simple adjustments, simple.

(Verse 3)

First, findin' all the rules of thumb,

Then mendin' any sores to numb.

Trackin' all causes known,

Crackin' all the effects just like stone.

Followin' the simplest algorithm,

The changes are set and all in rhythm.

(Chorus 3)

Simple adjustments were all that it took.

Page by page, my friends, they're all just simple books.

So simple adjustments were all that it took,

Simple adjustments, no matter how it looked.

Simple adjustments were all that it took.

Simple adjustments, simple.

Might Be Closer

[Verse 1]

If heaven was a place

Where everything was free,

It might be great for a while,

But what would great be worth?

With no work,

Playin' hide and go seek all day long,

With purpose and value.

And if the mark of hell is

The burden

Of suffering eternally,

Even a righteous man knows,

Hindsight can hurt like hellfire, too.

Once been wrong, though change has come,

Oh, but some scars stick around.

Once been wrong, change has come,

But some scars stick around.

[Chorus]

Heaven might be closer than I

Ever thought before,

But if it is,

Maybe Hell is, too.

Examining the bare bones truth,

Could be near or far,

But it's more like why and how

Than where we are.

Whether earning our eternities,

Or mortals chasing time that flees,

Good means good,

And need I add?

175

Whether earning our eternities,

Or mortals chasing time that flees,

Good means good,

And bad means bad.

[Verse 2]

What kind of God is ours?

That would set up an imperfect world,

Where the bad are free

To harm a soul living compassionately,

And have the gall to call it

A gauge of how we'd get along utopianly?

I wonder if he ever had to

Steal for a meal.

Said I wonder if he ever had to

Steal for a meal.

If he's perfect like they say,

Why would he treat this place like it's just a rough draft?

Second comings,

Armageddon,

You'd think he would have got it right the first time.

Second comings,

Armageddon,

You'd think he would have got it right the first time.

[Chorus]

Heaven might be closer than I

Ever thought before,

But if it is,

Maybe Hell is, too.

Examining the bare bones truth,

Could be near or far,

But it's more like why and how

Than where we are.

Whether earning our eternities,

Or mortals chasing time that flees,

Good means good,

And need I add?

Whether earning our eternities,

Or mortals chasing time that flees,

Good means good,

And bad means bad.

[Verse 3]

A Buddha's nature's curiously

Close to being heavenly,

But the Boddhisatvas' holy hearts are

A little closer to the broken parts.

Our wants can trick a soul to sadness,

Or harnessed navigate the madness,

But if heaven's not a state of mind, too,

You might just miss it if it finally finds you.

Yeah, a want can trick a soul to sadness,

Or harnessed navigate the madness,

But if heaven's not a state of mind, too,

You might just miss it

If it finally finds you.

Let The Rest Come Home

(Verse 1)

Wishin' my time was to tell by, not to be told by.

Least my rhyme is to know by, not to be known by,

And my eyes to see by, not to be seen by.

(Chorus 1)

Sometimes come out on top. Oh, every now and then, you flop.

So feel it out, don't stand too tall,And once you're ready, make your call.

177

'Cuz you got to bet and hold,To let the rest come home.

You got to bet and hold,To let the rest come,

Let the rest come,Let the rest come,

Let the rest come,Let the rest come home.

(Verse 2)

My mind is to think by, not to be thought by,

And my heart to beat by, not to be beat by.

Tryin' to make my fears to grow by, never to be grown by.

(Chorus 2)

Sometimes come out on top,Oh, every now and then, you flop.

So feel it out, don't stand too tall,And once you're ready, make your call.

'Cuz you got to bet and hold,To let the rest come home.

You got to bet and hold,To let the rest come,

Let the rest come,Let the rest come,

Let the rest come,Let the rest come home.

(Verse 3)

Love has been a dove and closer to a shove.

Love has shown me up, and love has shown me down.

Love has made me laugh, and love's made me the clown.

But I'm bettin' my, puttin' my bets on love.

(Bridge)

I'm bettin' my, puttin' my bets on love

I'm bettin' my, puttin' my bets on love

I'm bettin' my, puttin' my bets on love

I'm bettin' my, puttin' my bets on love

(Chorus 3)

Sometimes, come out on top, Oh, every now and then, you flop.

So feel it out, don't stand too tall,And once you're ready, make your call.

'Cuz you got to bet and hold,To let the rest come home.

You got to bet and hold,To let the rest come,

Let the rest come,Let the rest come,

Let the rest come. Let the rest come home

Walkin' On

(Verse 1)

Maybe sendin' different messages to different religions was a conscious decision,

But as of now, it proves to be the world's most divisive idealism schism.

And apparently, omnipotence did not stand a chance

When up against the need for there to be a need to eat.

But who am I to question a perfect entity?

But who is he to supply me with the fuel for mockery?

Said, who am I to question a perfect entity?

But who is he to supply me with the fuel for mockery?

(Chorus 1)

Expectin' to see God on television's

"Where are they now?"

Any day,

But anyway,

Guess I'll just keep walkin' on.

Expectin' to see God on television's

"Where are they now?"

Any day,

But anyway,

Guess I'll just keep walkin' on.

Keep walkin, got to keep walkin',

I got to, keep walkin' on.

(Verse 2)

So what's the deal with disease? How could he ever be at ease,

knowin' we didn't even have to sneeze?

Maybe terminal illness was his practical joke

on an unwittingly eternal folk.

But why natural disasters? I've got to ask you, master.

If you're not even down here to share the misery,

Makes me wonder 'bout your sense of sympathy.

179

But who am I to question a perfect entity?

But who is he, to supply me with the fuel for mockery?

Said, who am I to question a perfect entity?

But who is he, to supply me with the fuel for mockery?

(Chorus 2)

Expectin' to see God on television's

"Where are they now?"

Any day,

But anyway,

Guess I'll just

Keep walkin' on.

Expectin' to see God on television's

"Where are they now?"

Any day,

But anyway,

Guess I'll just keep walkin' on.

Send Me A Sign

(Verse 1)

I can see you lookin' from the other side of the room,

You can see me scopin' out the notion maybe we could be fine.

Maybe we could be fine, maybe we could be.

Mixin' signals like a DJ who just can't pick a song,

My heart just wriggles as my head plays along.

I can see you lookin' from the other side of the room,

You can see me scopin' out the notion maybe we could be fine.

Maybe we could be fine, maybe we could be.

(Chorus 1)

Won't you send me a sign,

Won't you please just let me know,

Could we be fine,

Or would you say "Yo"?

Won't you send me a sign,

Won't you please just let me know,

Could we be fine,

Or would you say "Yo"?

Could we be fine,

Or would you say "Yo"?

Could we be fine,

Or would you say "Yo"?

(Verse 2)

With all the vibes goin' around,

And some of the signals down,

I might love to tell the town,

But I wouldn't want to see you frown.

If you could clarify for me,

The suggestions I can see,

Anticipation's hesitations could finally be freed.

(Chorus 2)

Won't you send me a sign,

Won't you please just let me know,

Could we be fine,

Or would you say "Yo"?

Won't you send me a sign,

Won't you please just let me know,

Could we be fine,

Or would you say "Yo"?

Could we be fine,

Or would you say "Yo"?

Could we be fine,

Or would you say "Yo"?

Social Gravity

Social Gravity

Could the concept of free, possibly better be?
Washed way out to sea, than dictating our deeds?
Shouldn't matters of heart be, more like our destiny,
Then just buried inside, for our egos to ride?
Wild or tame, yeah, heavenly or blame,
If you went up in flames, I think it'd be a shame.

Will there be a time where peace and justice
don't just seem like a paradox?
It'd be so refined to see mankind be the kind of man you'd find.
A righteous state of mind doesn't really have to cost us all a dime.
If everyone was kind, utopia wouldn't be such a fantasy,
utopia wouldn't be such a fantasy,

utopia wouldn't be such a fantasy.

Do the holes and the ashes, of hellfire crashes?
Still seem cool to the classes, of up-and-coming badasses?
And would the souls of the masses, possibly better be,
With more sand dollar assets,
than lining the pockets of fat cat fur jackets?
Is this song in vain, because it causes pain?
Would you do your part, so things don't turn out lame?

Will there be a time where peace and justice
don't just seem like a paradox?
It'd be so refined to see mankind be the kind of man you'd find.
A righteous state of mind doesn't really have to cost us all a dime.
If everyone was kind, utopia wouldn't be such a fantasy,
utopia wouldn't be such a fantasy,
utopia wouldn't be such a fantasy.

Woke at Midnight

They say join the rat race,
I say save yo soul's face.
They say I'm a disgrace,
I say they'll be replaced.
Woke at midnight,
Others sleepin', dreamin',
They don't wanna waken
To the new day, I partake in.

Woke at midnight,
Broken wing flight,
New Age wanderer,
Old school ponderer.

183

It's a nice new day
Might go lay
Down the way
With my baby.

Sing my song
All night long,
Woke the folk,
Whose spirits choked.

Woke at midnight,
Broken wing flight,
New Age wanderer,
Old school ponderer.

It's a nice new day.
Might go lay
Down the way
With my baby.

Sing my song
All night long,
Woke the folk,
Whose spirits choked.

They say join the rat race,
I say save yo soul's face.
They say I'm a disgrace,
I say they'll be replaced.

Woke at midnight,
Others sleepin', dreamin',
They don't wanna waken
To the new day, I partake in.

Woke at midnight,
Broken wing flight,
New Age wanderin',
Old school ponderin'.

Electric Halo

I don't wanna be my own demon
'Cuz I'd be givin' myself hell.
And I don't wanna be just human,
'Cuz humane sounds twice as well.
But I can't be just selfless
Like those fairytales, they tell.
Fairytales, they tell,
Like those fairytales, they tell.

So sometimes I'm my own angel,
Sometimes electric halo.
Yeah, sometimes I'm my own angel,
I care because I'm able.

Can't always take the highest path,
Sometimes, gotta be down to Earth,
And the middle of the road
Ain't a very wise place to stay,
But chillin' in my basement's
'Bout as close to hell as I wanna be,
Far from hell as I wanna be,
As not in hell as I wanna be.

So sometimes I'm my own angel,
Sometimes Electric Halo.

185

Yeah, sometimes I'm my own angel,

I care because I'm able.

Saint's Dilemma

Saint Peter got a big ol' dilemma on his hands,

What the hell's he gonna do with a corpse in a box?

With another vampire in a box…

Saint Peter got a big ol' dilemma on his hands,

What the hell's he gonna do with a corpse in a box?

With another zombie in a box…

Singin'

More, More, More, More, More,

And it's never enough, it's never enough. Never singin'

More, more, more, more, more

And it's never enough, it's never enough. Never singin'

More, More, More

And their Zion isn't nothin' but a dream anymore.

Saint Patrick, with a big ol' dilemma on his hands,

What the hell's he gonna do with 'em callin' life luck, what the?

Callin' life luck, what the? Singin'

Saint Patrick with a big ol' dilemma on his hands,

What the hell's he gonna do with 'em callin' life luck, what the?

Callin' life luck, what the?

Singin'

More, More, More, More, More,

And it's never enough, it's never enough.

Singin'

More, More, More, More, More,

And it's never enough, it's never enough.

Singin' More, more, more,

And their Zion isn't nothin' but a dream anymore.

186

Saint Nick got a big ol' dilemma on his hands,

How's he gonna help karma deal its own cards?

Help karma deal its own cards…

Saint Nick got a big ol' dilemma on his hands,

How's he gonna help karma deal with its own cards?

Help karma deal its own cards…

Everybody's Singin'

More, More, More, More, More,

And it's never enough, never enough. Never Singin'

More, More, More, More, More,

And it's never enough, like give 'em more stuff, Never singin'

More, more, more,

And their Zion isn't nothin' but a dream anymore.

Saint Michael got a big ol' dilemma on his hands,

How's he gonna get 'em all to row their own boats ashore?

Get 'em all to row their own boats ashore…

Saint Michael got a big ol' dilemma on his hands,

How's he gonna get 'em all to row their own boats ashore?

Get 'em all to row their own boats ashore…

He's singin'

Row, row, row, row, row,

Merrily merrily merrily merrily merrily

He's singin'

Row, row, row, row, row,

Merrily merrily merrily merrily merrily

Row, Row, Row,

And their Zion isn't nothin' but a dream anymore.

Wisdom's Throne

Feet of stone, Mind as a sparrow,

My heart's a fire melting the ice.

Wisdom's throne's nev' too narrow,

And nothing's quite as nice,

Nothing's quite as nice.

Cuz in a freed world where everybody's doin' something,

Don't just feel how we want to, we get what we give.

In a free world where everybody's doin' something',

We don't just feel how we live, we get what they give.

We don't just feel how we want to, we get what we give,

We don't just feel how we live, we get what they give.

I see 'em all in groves of matter but far too few in those that matter,

Riddin' their garden groves of weeds, appearing in abundance,

Common masses of the fields, bred to clone their own redundance,

Wiser minds are led to find Buddha buds grow twice as kind,

Wiser minds are led to find Buddha buds grow twice as kind,

Cuz in a freed world where everybody's doin' something,

Don't just feel how we want no, we get what we give.

In a free world where everybody's doin' something',

We don't just feel how we live, we get what they give.

We don't just feel how we want to, we get what we give,

We don't just feel how we live, we get what they give.

Plantin' good seeds in perfect soil, but neglect could bring cause to toil,

So I'll get weeds small, one and all for tomorrow,

fosterin' my flowers to grow tall.

I'll be comin' home more joy than sorrow 'cause nothin' is quite as nice.

I'll be comin' home more joy than sorrow 'cause nothin' is quite as nice.

Cuz in a freed world where everybody's doin' something,

Don't just feel how we want no, we get what we give.

In a free world where everybody's doin' something',

We don't just feel how we live, we get what they give.

We don't just feel how we want to, we get what we give,

We don't just feel how we live, we get what they give.

Rise Up in Love

Honey, oh, the shame, a selfish man exclaims.

He wants her all for him, he's calling' that more tame.

He teaches kids to share could teach himself the same.

Another follows her lust, so her head is hard to trust.

Her self-control's a bust, so her heart is wrapped in rust.

Wonder why they call it fallin' in love,

'Cuz if there's fallin' in love it's just 'cuz it ain't gettin' done right.

So all we got to do is rise up in love,

'Cuz when it's really pure love, it ain't no fall it's just a flight.

Wonder why they call it fallin' in love,

'Cuz when there's fallin' in love it's just 'cuz it ain't gettin' done right.

So all we got to do is rise up in love,

'Cuz when it's really pure love, it ain't no fall it's just a flight.

Fightin' every night, then tryin' to make things right,

A roller coaster ride with contradicting sides.

They say it's in the plan, they get burnt, then tan.

Another waits by the phone, it's not alone to roam,

So there's a price to pay for all of them today.

Wonder why they call it fallin' in love,

'Cuz if there's fallin' in love, it's just 'cuz it ain't gettin' done right.

So all we got to do is rise up in love,

'Cuz when it's really pure love, it ain't no fall it's just a flight.
Wonder why they call it fallin' in love,
'Cuz if there's fallin' in love it's just 'cuz it ain't gettin' done right.
So all we got to do is rise up in love,
'Cuz when it's really true love, it ain't no fall it's just a flight.

With no get, no give, their normal way to live,
Some miss the gourmet shelf, it's risen above the self,
On the brightest days, just givin' it all away
Yeah, on the brightest days, just givin' it all away
'Cuz the best love we got for ya comes with no charge at all.
The best love we got comes with no charge at all.

Wonder why they call it fallin' in love,
'Cuz if there's fallin' in love, it's just 'cuz it ain't gettin' done right.
So all we got to do is rise up in love,
'Cuz when it's really pure love, it ain't no fall it's just a flight.
Wonder why they call it fallin' in love,
'Cuz if there's fallin' in love it ain't gettin' done right,
it ain't gettin' done right.
So all we got to do is rise up in love,
'Cuz when it's really pure love, it ain't no fall it's just a flight.
All we got to do is rise up in love,
'Cuz when it's really pure love, it ain't no fall it's just a flight.
It's just a flight, it's just a flight, it's just a flight.

All we got to do is rise up in love,
'Cuz when it's really pure love, it ain't no fall it's just a flight.

Righteously Sublime

Wishin' their days weren't glazed in a melancholy haze.

Thankful my ways weren't designed by the modern-day maze.

A thousand times through, but it only takes a moment of Zen,

To bring 'em right 'round

where their hearts are guardians of unstruck sounds,

Where their hearts are guardians of our heads.

When our minds put the my to the side,

our eyes can see right between the lines,

Far as them lovin' feelings fly, our hearts can decipher an ego's disguise,

or an ego's lies.

When a mind puts the my to the side, a soul's that righteously sublime.

If your mind puts the my behind, your soul's that righteously sublime.

Time freezes like a snowflake caught in the wind,

Space echoes from without just as from within,

Cause dances round in paradoxes woven with effects,

For the moment, when we're for the moment,

we feel the harmony of bein' free.

When our minds put the my to the side,

our eyes can see right between the lines,

Far as them lovin' feelings fly, our hearts can decipher an ego's disguise,

or our hearts can decipher an ego's lies.

When a mind puts the my to the side, a soul's that righteously sublime.

If your mind puts the my behind, your soul's that righteously sublime.

Transcendental just like mountains risin' up above the clouds,

Deep submarinin', souls periscopin' all the surface scenes.

Meditative missions, overflowin' with riches,

But if you're full of self, then ya just can't hold 'em,

there's no room to hold 'em.

So we're holdin' our highest hands our friends,

followin' their commands, and then we're

Walkin' the Buddha land again and again and again and again.

When a mind puts the my to the side, a soul's that righteously sublime.

When a mind puts the my to the side,

our eyes can see right between the lines,

Far as them lovin' feelings fly,

our hearts can decipher an ego's disguise

or an ego's lies.

If a mind puts the my right behind, a soul's that righteously sublime.

When a mind puts the my to the side, a soul's that righteously sublime.

Alternative Phenomenon

‘Round the Block

One thing I learned about the path of descent,
One false move, and you can't even pay the rent, na na.
The thing that struck me 'bout the cave down low,
There's a reason why the grass don't grow.
The thing I learned about the way on up,
The work's as worth it as it fills the cup.
A little note about being' on top,

The light's as bright as heaven's might, so it can keep you in flight, yeah.

It could take a whole trip 'round the block back to that same ol' clock,

To finally hear it tick-tock, like it don't care if you like it or not.

So, from the past, I try to gleam a trophy case of the mistakes,

And let 'em replace future days

laced with lessons not learned from the taste

Tick tock, it doesn't care if you lack it or not,

Tick tock, it doesn't care if you like it or not.

I been up that creek, I used my hands to paddle.

I been so down to earth, it's like I was made of salt.

I been left for dead just like a funeral parlor

But I was right all along about love been' so good for us.

It could take a whole trip 'round the block back to that same ol' clock,

To finally hear it tick-tock, like it don't care if you like it or not.

So, from the past, I try to gleam a trophy case of the mistakes,

And let 'em replace future days

laced with lessons not learned from the taste

Tick tock, it doesn't care if you lack it or not,

Tick tock, it doesn't care if you like it or not.

Never Clip Your Wings (Robyn)

I saw you flying 'round, just the other day in a special way.

The way you moved along, the way you sung your song,

it inspired me to say,

I hope we meet again, I hope I make you grin,

I hope that life works out your way.

I truly do, my friend, hope this is not the end,

'cuz it would be too soon for me.

194

I would never clip your wings. I'd just love to hear you sing.

Your lovin's like a song to me, a sweet melody indeed.

I would never clip your wings; I'd just love to hear you sing.

Your lovin's like a song to me, a sweet melody indeed.

You don't belong in a cage; songbirds like you are all the rage.

You belong in a symphony, singin' lead for the people to see.

I'd help you with your cause to fret; bear hug's rough as I would get.

So if you're in the mood for a sing-along,

with love like ours, yeah, we can't go wrong.

I would never clip your wings; I'd just love to hear you sing.

Your lovin's like a song to me, a sweet melody indeed.

I would never clip your wings; I'd just love to hear you sing.

Your lovin's like a song to me, a sweet melody indeed.

Fantasy Woman

She can hang with the boys,

She don't destroy children's toys.

She's pretty drama free,

'Cuz she's as wise as she can be.

She keeps a cool head in matters of thought,

And comes from the heart, for those that are not.

Once in a while, she'd just see me and smile.

Every now and then, she'd say, "You're my good friend" again.

She's my fantasy woman, my fantasy woman,

In the middle of a not-so-fantasy world.

Fantasy woman in the middle of a not-so-fantasy world.

Fantasy woman, fantasy woman, in the middle of a not-so-fantasy world.

195

She's not shallow or vain, yeah,

And she deals with the pain, yeah.

She's not real materialistic,

And won't weigh me by my paycheck.

She's not afraid of the dirt,

Or wearin' a skirt, yeah.

She might not be the cleanest,

But she's the opposite of meanest.

She never plays me like games,

Takes me in when it rains, yeah.

She knows about the dark,

But she loves the light, yeah.

She's my fantasy woman, my fantasy woman,

In the middle of a not-so-fantasy world.

Fantasy woman, in the middle of a not-so-fantasy world.

Fantasy woman, fantasy woman, in the middle of a not-so-fantasy world.

Learn or Burn

Like a magnet for repair, despair can demand our care.

Like a call to a higher ground, a crisis' scream can sound.

Like fuel for a warm embrace, can be a lonely, tear-strewn face.

Moonshine at sundown, dreams done by sunrise.

The cause for our concern can present the chance to learn or burn.

Like if the things we don't want at all

Are the reasons that we stood so tall,

Or the things that some want most

Can just turn their soul to a ghost.

To learn or burn to learn or burn.

Like the drugs that they thought they'd love

That just haunted them through the night.

Like that one last one-night stand that just left them in a doctor's hands.

Like opposites that detract, with the facts you wish you could subtract.

Moonshine at sundown, dreams done by sunrise.

The cause for our concern can present the chance to learn or burn.

Like if the things we don't want at all

Are the reasons that we stood so tall,

Or the things that some want most can just turn their soul to a ghost.

To learn or burn to learn or burn.

Mirage

Sometimes the surface gleams, but underneath it teems,

Surprises ranged from vile to the wildly obscene.

Whatever's comin' next sheathed by guises that just seem,

Oases phantoms stealin' all the sentient scenes.

Makin' love to a mirage, but sittin' back to wonder,

Reality's barrage sheds light upon the blunder.

Makin' love to a mirage, but sittin' back to wonder,

Reality's barrage, full of lightning and thunder.

Tossin' pennies in a well might make your dreams come true,

But donate one to hell, might make your nightmares, too.

Spent a fortune on an epic fantasy,

But fortune, it would seem, could fool you epically.

Makin' love to a mirage, but sittin' back to wonder,

Reality's barrage sheds light upon the blunder.

Makin' love to a mirage, but sittin' back to wonder,

Reality's barrage, full of lightning and thunder.

Accidentally

Accidentally this mornin', woke up up in heaven next to god.

Accidentally this afternoon, got a 5-0 beatdown in the park.

Accidentally this evenin', Laid my head to rest without a nod.

Tiptoein' callin' 'em accidents, But the snow was fallin' on my tent.

Tiptoein' callin' 'em accidents, bet the blizzard's why you paid your rent.

All this, tiptoein' callin' 'em accidents,

while the reason's seeming clear as day to you.

Accidentally this mornin', woke up as a member of the institution.

Accidentally this afternoon, found the gates of heaven are our hearts.

Accidentally this evenin', checked myself right out, never goin' back.

Tiptoein' callin' 'em accidents, But the snow was fallin' on my tent.

Tiptoein' callin' 'em accidents, bet the blizzard's why you paid your rent.

All this, tiptoein' callin' 'em accidents,

while the reason's seeming clear as day to me.

Tiptoein' callin' 'em accidents, But the snow was fallin' on my tent.

Tiptoein' callin' 'em accidents, bet the blizzard's why you paid your rent.

No more tiptoein' callin' 'em accidents,

'Cuz the reason's screaming clear as day to me.

Accidentally this mornin', woke up back down here on the planet Earth.

Accidentally this afternoon, once again was glad my mom gave birth.

Accidentally this evenin', laid my head to rest without a qualm.

Modern Mystic

Far as I can tell, God's like a ghost,

Known by messengers and signs that he posts.

Seems to be, nature's only got half a clue,

With quantum riddles and its mysteries true as blue.

Science seems to say, nothin's got a mind of its own,

Particles appearin' near and far just like the dice were rolled.

Could it be, that a mystery's just part of how it be?

Could that be, why the more we see, the more blind we can be?

Could it be, that a mystery's just part of how it be?

Could that be, why the more we see, the more blind we can be?

Far as I can tell, God's like a ghost,

Known by messengers and sign that he posts.

Seems to be, nature's only got half a clue,

With quantum riddles and its mysteries true as blue.

Science seems to say, nothin's got a mind of its own,

Particles appearin' near and far just like the dice were rolled.

Could it be, that a mystery's just part of how it be?

Could that be, why the more we see, the more blind we can be?

Could it be, that a mystery's just part of how it be?

Could that be, why the more we see, the more blind we can be?

Minin' Silver Linin's

It's been one of those years where I make lots of lemonade.
Sometimes, it feels like lemons were the only fruit for sale at all.
There's been some of them tears, the kind that shake a soul right straight.
Time's been screamin' my ear off, there's been altogether too much hate.
Pickin' up the pieces of a tattered life, born again and again unto strife.
Pickin' up the pieces of a tattered life, born again and again unto strife.

Minin' Silver linin's like they were the fuel for shinin'.
Diggin' down deep for somethin' way up in the sky.
Minin' silver linin's like they were the fuel for smilin',
Mindful that the weather's gonna sway someday.

I like to think things happen for a reason,
but sometimes I have to wonder why.
Misfortune sets my head a frickin' spinnin',
like justice, has just passed me by.
I know 'cause of some facts of life, some suffering is guaranteed, yeah,
But why on Earth should anybody suffer
at the hand of someone's foolish creed?
Why on Earth should anybody suffer
at the hand of someone's foolish creed?

Minin' Silver linin's like they were the fuel for shinin'.
Diggin' down deep for somethin' way up in the sky.
Minin' silver linin's like they were the fuel for smilin',
Mindful that the weather's gonna sway someday.

Nameless Epiphany

I have been a money-hungry capitalist, and my greed soon took its toll.

Dreamt of bein' an idealistic communist, but it empties out your bowl.

Thought it'd be cool to be an anarchist,

but not when chaos kills more than control.

Tried to be an isolationist, but my life was too lonely in a hole.

A little too lonely in a little too lonely in a hole.

So here comes a sarcastic plea,

Isn't there a stereotype for me?

Wadin' in nomenclature up to my knees,

Waitin' on a nameless epiphany.

Wadin' in nomenclature up to my knees,

Waitin' on a nameless epiphany.

Waitin' on a nameless epiphany.

Felt the emptiness of the nihilist, nearly hollowed out my soul.

Seen the black and white lights of the Zen Buddhist,

but balance is just one role.

My two eyes have seen just a little bit more than they'd have liked to see,

and I've been stifled by my range.

Thought I'd love to be a realist,

But even that's an abstract goal.

So what damn good is this philosophic list,

If it don't leave me feelin' whole?

It didn't leave me feelin', it didn't leave me feelin' whole.

So here comes a sarcastic plea,

Isn't there a stereotype for me?

Wadin' in nomenclature up to my knees,

Waitin' on a nameless epiphany.

Wadin' in nomenclature up to my knees,

Waitin' on a nameless epiphany.

Waitin' on a nameless epiphany.

So here comes a sarcastic plea,
Isn't there a stereotype for me?
Wadin' in nomenclature up to my knees,
Waitin' on a nameless epiphany.
Waitin' on a nameless epiphany.
Waitin' on a nameless, waitin' on a nameless epiphany.

Raised

Chasing inner silence, done slaughtered inner peace.
Raising interference on the Godliest of meats,
My wounded flesh was royalty,
My mind was flushed right out to sea.

In the heat of the moment, my soul was ablaze,
As the flight of the phoenix, my essence was raised.
And with bittersweet timing, my mind was uncaged.
And with bittersweet timing, my mind was uncaged.

My soul paroled, my eyes could see
The shotty shackles I called me,
From far outside the standard scene,
So far removed, it was a dream.
It was all a dream.
Insanity's sweet, supple song
Played on orchestral rusty gongs.

In the heat of the moment, my soul was ablaze,
As the flight of the phoenix, my essence was raised.
And with bittersweet timing, my mind was uncaged.

And with bittersweet timing, my mind was uncaged.

Wrapped up in living lucidly, my body caged but spirit-free,
A silent footstep treads my head, and quiet glee comes over me.
The war was o'er, I need not flee.
Bout time 'cause my soul was as good as dead.

Enlightening as a Feather

So fly away now, Mr. Bluebird, fly away now, Mrs. Black.
So fly away now, all of you, birds, Nev' to ever come back.

'Cause it's been a long day for the children,
It's been a longer day for the truth.
It's been a long day in this building,
Such a long rainy day with no roof.

'Cause the West sees no deeper than an ego's self-deception.
Some stay afloat on image rafts, and some drown in the illusions.

So fly away now now now, Mr. Bluebird, fly away now, Mrs. Black.
So fly away now, all of you, birds, Nev' to ever come back.
So fly away now, all of you, birds, Nev' to ever come back.

Oh, so I emptied out my cup of all those things I thought to be,
And I realized full cups fit no more of fleeting life's infinity.
And now I have a filling time, not busy filling all the time.

There's clean cups by the kitchen sink,
So come and join me, humble friends.
There's more than you and I could think,
Oh, that we'll see before the end.
With empty ears, you can hear it clear,

203

I say the truth speaks silently.

So you can stay now, Mr. Bluebird, you can stay now, Mrs. Black.
So you can stay now, all of you, birds, my jealousy ain't nev' to come back.
So you can stay now, all of you, birds, my jealousy ain't nev' to ev' ever come back.

Prism

Atheists treat science like it's their religion,
Observing the results just like the real world's petitions.
Agnostics not sure what to make of the scene,
Acknowledging the mysteries in what has been seen.
Pagans sayin' nature is all that we see,
And they got a point with that one naturally.
Buddhists gettin' right to the core of it all,
Right livin' definin' their deeds small and tall.

White light shone through a prism,
The real world, seemin' full of schisms.
Colored points each viewpoint has got,
To see clear, could we connect the dots?

White light shone through a prism,
The real world, seemin' full of schisms.
Colored points each viewpoint has got,
To see clear, should we connect the dots? Yeah.

Jews prove their God with their Exodus,
But still could use a save, just like the rest of us.
The Christian Messiah did some miracles,
Which least doesn't seem like they're just seein' molehills.
Islam's got the word of their God himself,
To clarify 'cause human hands had tainted his wealth.

Hindus have Gods that have power to share,
More like you'd expect from supreme beings who care.

White light shone through a prism,
The real world, seemin' full of schisms.
Colored points each viewpoint has got,
To see clear, could we connect the dots?

White light shone through a prism,
The real world, seemin' full of schisms.
Colored points each viewpoint has got,
To see clear, should we connect the dots? Yeah.

The Sound

I clear the dust from my boots,
And I mend the trust in my roots.
Mighta got torn, beaten down, or shaken up,
I'm born once again with a brimming cup.

I can hear the sound of fortune comin' around, yeah,
It's comin' around, yeah, yeah.
Not too long ago, some mighta thought it'd never show,
But ear down to the ground, could hear it comin' 'cross the town.
I had to get low to know, but now it's sure to show.
Reap and sow, they say, is bound to grow,
Seek, and so I say, be found to show.
It's comin' around, yeah,
It's comin' around, yeah yeah.

That past loosens up on it's grip,
The future is bright 'cause it won't slip.
The now ebbs along so gracefully,

Somehow, good things are happenin' for me.

I can hear the sound of fortune comin' around yeah,
It's comin' around, yeah yeah.
Not too long ago, some mighta thought it'd never show,
But ear down to the ground, could hear it comin' 'cross the town.
I had to get low to know, but now it's sure to show.
It's comin' around, yeah,
It's comin' around
Reap and sow, they say, is bound to grow,
Seek, and so I say, be found to show.
It's comin' around, yeah,
It's comin' around
It's comin' around, yeah,
It's comin' around

That sun is shinin' brighter today.
That sky's crystal clear as the way.
That ground's cushioned footsteps refuse to pound.
That air's clean as nature just found.

I can hear the sound of fortune comin' around yeah,
It's comin' around, yeah yeah.
Not too long ago, some mighta thought it'd never show,
But ear down to the ground, could hear it comin' 'cross the town.
I had to get low to know, but now it's sure to show.
It's comin' around, yeah, It's comin' around
Reap and sow, they say, is bound to grow,
Seek, and so I say, be found to show.
It's comin' around, yeah,
It's comin' around
It's comin' around, yeah,
It's comin' around

Metaphysical Sherpa:

Dirty Fractal Sacrament

TranscenDance in the Rain
(Greener)

By Nick Mirisola

Featuring G. Love

There's another way out tonight,

But looks like there might be a fight.

Instead of just gettin' it right,

You fuss around with all of your might.

Instead of just playin' the fool,

I'm gonna try to give you a tool.

If you let the rain train your brain,

You won't be seein' things the same.

You tryin'a move aside the seas, just to get rid of the rain.

Tryin'a override the tides, just to get rid of the pain.

If that's what you think that you got to do,

There's one thing that I wish you knew.

The rain may bring pain but there's somethin' to gain,

When your grass is greener than you ever seen.

And while that dark may rule the night,

It makes the sunlight seem so bright.

(Verse 2 by G. Love)

So you think you're the only one

That's ever been pushed down with their face in the ground?

Am I talkin' to myself too much?

I'm just tryin' to make sense of it all.

What's this life but a chance for learnin',

What's tomorrow but a chance to get it done?

I'mma get it done.

But I shouldn't have to be so frustrated,

The journey's there, that's the livin', that's the fun.

But I know that I can be better,

Yes I know I can feel it more,

Open up my heart,

Open up like the sky.

You tryin'a move aside the seas, just to get rid of the rain.

Tryin'a override the tides, just to get rid of the pain.

If that's what you think that you got to do,

There's one thing that I wish you knew.

The rain may bring pain but there's somethin' to gain,

When your grass is greener than you ever seen.

And while that dark may rule the night,

It makes the sunlight seem so bright

Nuke the Sun

You could try to teach a saint to take, or a tyrant to say please,

You could try but even Bob would tell ya,

It's gonna take a whole lotta whacks with that small little axe.

You could try to guide a Zen master, or snuff blind faith with facts,

You could try but if the light was just right,

An eye that isn't open all the way could be fuelin' the fight.

Yeah an eye that isn't open all the way could be foolin' the sight.

So I say you can't nuke the sun,

Nah nah nah nah you can't nuke the sun.

Well you can, but it's kinda like

Threatenin' a criminal on the run.

So I say you can't nuke the sun,

Nah nah nah nah you can't nuke the sun.

Well you can, but it's kinda like
Threatenin' a hero with a loaded gun.
So I say you can't nuke the sun,
Nah nah nah nah you can't nuke the sun.

You could try to give a demon hell, or sell an angel wings.
You could try but if they even let you,
The biggest loss of all's your lack of grace, as you're losin' some face.
You could try to save a church from dogma,
or a rich man from his greed.
You could try but closed minds can't decipher
their causes from their creeds.

So I say you can't nuke the sun,
Nah nah nah nah you can't nuke the sun.
Well you can, but it's kinda like
Threatenin' a criminal on the run.
So I say you can't nuke the sun,
Nah nah nah nah you can't nuke the sun.
Well you can, but it's kinda like
Threatenin' a hero with a loaded gun.
So I say you can't nuke the sun,
Nah nah nah nah you can't nuke the sun.

Indigo Perspective

I know indigo roses, all around,
Indigo petals paint the ground.
I know indigo children, all around,
Indigo footsteps paint the ground.
You try to keep us down,
You're only fuelin' your frown.
We pick each other up instead.

210

Yeah we let each other live,

'Cause we got, we got light to give.

We can illuminate the living dead.

Sometimes we illuminate the ungratefully dead.

Love's our spirit guide,

It's always by our side.

It's our spirit guide,

It's always by our side.

It's our spirit guide,

It's always by our side.

So we let the snow fall wildly all around us,

And the joy run gently 'round our face,

And the sun come up when the hell it wants to,

And the moon shine bright as it wants all night.

We see the naked you,

It casts an aura blue.

It come directly from the source of the true.

We see it there in you,

You get to glowin' too.

I know indigo roses, all around,

Indigo petals paint the ground.

I know indigo children, all around,

Indigo footsteps paint the ground.

You try to keep us down,

You're only fuelin' your frown.

We pick each other up instead.

Yeah we let each other live,

'Cause we got, we got light to give.

We can illuminate the living dead.

Sometimes we illuminate the ungratefully dead.

Love's our spirit guide,

It's always by our side.

It's our spirit guide,

It's always by our side.

It's our spirit guide,

It's always by our side.

So we let the snow fall wildly all around us,

And the joy run gently 'round our face,

And the sun come up when the hell it wants to,

And the moon shine bright as it wants all night.

Just say Om

As I wonder about my pain,

Acceptance comes on like a train,

Tied to the tracks or comin' out of the rain,

Either way it'll never be the same.

Tied to the tracks or comin' out of the rain,

Either way it'll never be the same.

Sometimes it hits me like a stone, stone, stone,

So I just say Om I just say Om I just say Om I just say.

And when I don't know where in the hell to go,

I just go home I just go home I just go home I just go.

So when it hits me like a stone, stone, stone,

So I just say Om I just say Om I just say Om I just say.

And when I don't know where in the hell to go,

I just go home I just go home I just go home I just go.

Pissed off again at the sound of the wind.

It's howlin' on down my neck it's,

Howlin' down, I'm a wreck and,

Thoughts are bubblin' up from the depths of my psyche.

After what I been through feel just a bit like Nike.

Marathon and on and on and on on,

Would it ever be gone,

Ever be gone?

Marathon and on and on and on on,

Would it ever be gone,

Ever be gone?

Sometimes it hits me like a stone, stone, stone,

So I just say Om I just say Om I just say Om I just say.

And when I don't know where in the hell to go,

I just go home I just go home I just go home I just go.

So when it hits me like a stone, stone, stone,

I just say Om I just say Om I just say Om I just say.

And when I don't know where in the hell to go,

I just go home I just go home I just go home I just go.

So when it hits me like a stone, stone, stone,

I just say Om, I just say Om, I just say Om, I just say Om.

Simpler Positivity

A little stability and a bucket o' joy

Go a whole long way in this messed up world,

But under a waterfall your bucket won't stand tall.

Mine's fallen too many times to ignore bliss' crimes.

Every time that I'm done and I'm wantin' to go home,

Bucket is gone and my chances are blown.

I stopped searchin' for bliss and set my sights on a simpler positivity.

It's not the top o' my list, 'cause well you get the gist,

213

Seemed to lead to escape or pain.

Escape or pain,

Escape or pain,

Escape or pain.

I need the type of approach that'll grow good times,

But won't knock my soul out of line.

The type that leaves us smilin' while we're passin' the while,

But leaves our futures fine.

Sometimes a little too much is a whole lot worse

Than a moderate take on even bliss' turf.

Sometimes a little too much is a whole lot worse

Than a moderate take on even bliss' turf.

I stopped searchin' for bliss and set my sights on a simpler positivity.

It's not the top o' my list, 'cause well you get the gist,

Seemed to lead to escape or pain.

Escape or pain,

Escape or pain,

Escape or pain.

Dear Jihadist

Dear Jihadist, yeah, please don't miss this, nah

I had a Muslim friend of mine, once say to me one time,

The internal Jihad is the higher of the paths,

So 'stead of fights externally, won't you come pray with me.

If your God's good as they do say,

He'd probably want the higher way.

Do you see Allah terrorizin'?

If your temperature is risin',

214

Warm your heart and not your head please.

Rather than war externally,

Long lost brothers we could be,

In a spiritual family.

Yeah I don't see Allah terrorizin',

So if your temperature is risin',

Warm your heart and not your head please,

Long lost brothers we could be,

In a spiritual family.

Dear Jihadist, yeah, please don't miss this, nah.

That Muslim friend of mine, once said to me another time,

"One meaning of Islam is Peace,"

So won't you demonstrate this please?

More helpful prayin' on your knees,

Than lyin' in a grave.

Not supposed to expect miracles,

But you bomb martyrs like you do.

Do you see Allah terrorizin'?

If your temperature is risin',

Warm your heart and not your head please.

Rather than war externally,

Long lost brothers we could be,

In a spiritual family.

Yeah I don't see Allah terrorizin',

So if your temperature is risin',

Warm your heart and not your head please,

Long lost brothers we could be,

In a spiritual family.

Dear Jihadist, yeah, please don't miss this, nah.

Both sides see extreme enemies,

Lost in their ideologies.

Could we just build a bridge instead,

Of burnin' 'em and countin' dead?

A foe will surely bring you woe,

But friends can broken fences mend.

If your God's good as they do say,

He'd probably want the higher way.

Do you see Allah terrorizin'?

If your temperature is risin',

Warm your heart and not your head please.

Rather than war externally,

Long lost brothers we could be,

In a spiritual family.

Yeah I don't see Allah terrorizin',

So if your temperature is risin',

Warm your heart and not your head please,

Long lost brothers we could be,

In a spiritual family.

Love Enough

I don't hate them politicians or their misleadin' eyes.

I just hate the greed, lies, and corruption that they supply.

I don't hate them actresses who sell themselves as sex.

I just hate the screen machine that profits on the vex.

I don't even hate them businessman tryin' to rape my mind for gold.

I just hate the system that instilled it, truth be told.

Oh truth be told.

But I don't hate the people of this money makin' hell because I know

When they're creatin' well, well, well,

creation ain't ever ever ever already well.

And I don't have to hate them no I know

They hate enough themselves.

And I don't have to hate them no no no no,

I can love enough myself.

I can love enough my self.

I 'm gonna love enough myself.

Seems like the system let one rip and tried to sell it to the flies.

Well won't it be surprised when they start buzzin' 'round its lies.

'Cause I've seen demons dressed in white, and singin' choir hymns.

I wonder if they're still church polite

when they're fulfilling their dark whims.

But I don't even hate those skeevy priests, done sippin' tainted wine.

I just hate that the powers that be crucify our bright young minds.

I just hate that the powers that be crucify our bright young minds.

But I don't hate the people of this God foresaken hell because I know

When they're creatin' well well, creation ain't ever ever already well.

And I don't have to hate them no I know

They hate enough themselves.

And I don't have to hate them no no no no,

I can love enough myself.

I don't have to hate them no no no,

I can love enough my self.

Not Losin' Out

Next time you're feelin' like the world's comin' down on you,

And you're worn down by the weight,

Brothers and sisters remember this,

I'm here to help you through.

I'm here to help you through.

Let's let loneliness get lost,

Sympathize our search,

217

Freedom be our finding.

Lettin' every line be crossed,

Every crime be tossed,

Without love losin' out.

Nah nah without love losin' out.

I ain't gonna let our love lose out,

I ain't gonna let our love lose.

Sometimes we just don't know what to do.

Everything we think of is tainted blue.

When I'm feelin' worn down and lonely too,

At least there'll be sunshine when we're, sunshine when through.

At least there'll be sunshine when we're, sunshine when we're through.

Let's let loneliness get lost,

Sympathize our search,

Freedom be our finding.

Lettin' every line be crossed,

Every crime be tossed,

Without love losin' out.

Nah nah without love losin' out.

I ain't gonna let our love lose out,

I ain't gonna let our love lose.

Lap Dance (Behind the Poles)
Featuring Killah Priest

Verse 1:

(Audio Lyrics by Killah Priest)

Verse 2 (Lyrics by Meditative Animal):

Now I don't wanna pay to play, or roll in the hay,

Swing, sway, or seize the day.

Romance lances a chance,

For a fancier dance,

Or a France trance prance,

That I commance with a glance.

But I'm not here to judge, or hold no grudge.

In fact I don't even think that stick could use a smudge.

And I ain't even ever been to a strip joint,

But I've made love to strippers and I get the point.

I like her tiger style,

She makes my lion roar.

But I don't objectify just to erectify,

Some need to rectify, before they wreck the high.

Now I'm not sayin' you can't have some fun,

Hell I really hope you have a ton.

Just remember there are hearts and souls

Behind the twerks and poles.

Chorus 1:

'Cause there are hearts and souls behind the twerks and poles.

There are hearts and souls behind the twerks and poles.

There are hearts and souls behind the twerks and poles.

There are hearts and souls…

219

Verse 3 (Meditative Animal):

Bodhidharma comin' at ya like a farmah o' the karma.

Reap and sowin', seeds be growin', garden got me on alarmah.

Zang Sanfeng sang to Shaolin a Tai Chi symphony in me.

Jivin' 'bout the Pu-Tang with Wu-Tang.

I'm Just a lay zen monk showing ya how we do hang.

The thing is that the whole world really is a temple,

Shaolin just act like it, the rest of you is mental.

Chorus 2:

'Cause there are hearts and souls behind the robes and poles.

There are hearts and souls behind the robes and poles.

Shredded It So Much Better

Some mellow blue,

And some well placed red.

Some yellow too

To light your head.

Well it mighta been a masterpiece it's true,

But now it looks like you been wastin' yo time instead.

'Cause well you paint a pretty picture,

But you shredded it so much better.

What can a thousand words be worth

In pieces on the floor?

What can a thousand words be worth

In pieces on the floor?

Each stroke was thoughtful and from the heart.

Emotions ran but still ran smart.

Well it mighta been a masterpiece it's true,
But now it looks like you been wastin' yo time instead.

'Cause well you paint a pretty picture,
But you shredded it so much better.
What can a thousand words be worth
In pieces on the floor?
What can a thousand words be worth
In pieces on the floor?
Pieces on,
On the floor.
In scattered pieces on the floor.

Aftermath
(Oh My Rappah's Sanity)
Featuring Sticky Fingaz

Verse 1:

(Audio lyrics by Sticky Fingaz)

Chorus 1: (By Meditative Animal)

Om Ah Ra Pa Tsa Na Dhih
Om Ah Ra Pa Tsa Na Dhih
Om Ah Ra Pa Tsa Na Dhih
Like oh my rappah's sanity.
Om Ah Ra Pa Tsa Na Dhih
Chantin' Om Ah Ra Pa Tsa Na Dhih
Like oh my rappah's sanity.

Verse 2: (By Meditative Animal)

Some call me Manjushri

That was my mantra seed.

Practicin' my Tai Chi

Just like a Bodhi tree.

I'm just a Bodhisattva Shambala souljah

Cuttin' through ignorance

Just like dry house plants.

Sword iconography

Just like Shaolin see

Rainin' down lightnin' for Heavenly victory.

I'm chantin' Om Ah Ra Pa Tsa Na Dhih

Like oh my rappah's sanity.

I'm chantin' Om Ah Ra Pa Tsa Na Dhih

Like oh my rappah's sanity.

Om Ah Ra Pa Tsa Na Dhih

Om Ah Ra Pa Tsa Na Dhih

Om Ah Ra Pa Tsa Na Dhih

Om Ah Ra Pa Tsa Na Dhih

Soul Reckoning

Waves, crashing on the beach,

Knowledge lying out of reach,

I heard a storm move through last night,

This morning could blocked out sunlight.

Do I even want to know,

Which way the seed of life will grow?

Where are we headed?

Wherever your head is.

What should we know?

Which way to grow.

What's in store?

Is the price much more?

Eternity beckons,

My soul, ready, reckons.

A hint of mysticism,

And a dash of cold hard truth.

If darkness comes my way,

At least I know my hearts glows through.

A fact or two may miss the ride,

So may wisdom be my faithful guide.

Where are we headed?

Wherever your head is.

What should we know?

Which way to grow.

What's in store?

Is the price much more?

Eternity beckons,

My soul, ready, reckons.

An Ode Will Have to Do (Om Ma Ma)

Verse 1: (Lyrics by Nick Mirisola)

I guess an ode will have to do.

Just like your ashes in a sea of blue.

We never got our big duet,

But I just cannot forget,

So sing along to your own song,

In an angel voice now ever long.

Feel free to visit in our dreams,

So it's not as far as it seems.

Yeah ma this one is for you,

I'm just singin' it for two.

Heart of gold, a headstrong warrior,

Your love still transcends every barrier.

Om ma ma

Om ma ma ma ma ma ma ma ma ma ma

Om ma ma ma ma ma ma ma ma ma ma

Om ma ma

Ma ma ma ma ma ma ma ma ma ma

Verse 2: (Lyrics by John Dixon Mirisola)

A little kid with pots and pans,

A teenage misfit with his

Basement punk rock band-

You never even said a word

With all that music

Pounding up through the floor.

So I've got one more tune to show you,

Just like those mornings

You would drive me to school:

A simple ballad by your boys,

The ones you let make all that

Ever loving noise.

Om ma ma

Om ma ma ma ma ma ma ma ma ma

Om ma ma

Om ma ma

Lighter Route

I'm hangin' in there.
Maybe not up on top,
But I'm hangin' in there,
Maybe not by a lot,
But I'm hangin' in there,
And it's clear to see,
I'm not lettin' go.
No I'm not lettin' go
I'm not lettin' go.

Sometimes when I'm about to pout,
I try to find a lighter route,
And give it a little time
To work itself on out.
Sometimes when I'm about to pout,
I try to find a lighter route,
And give it a little time
To work itself on out.
Sometimes when I'm about to pout,
I try to find a lighter route,
And give it a little time
To work itself on out.
Sometimes when I'm about to pout,
I try to find a lighter route,
And give it a little time
To work itself on out.
Jokin' and foolin' are handy tools,
'Cause how you're glowin', Heaven's knowin'.
So drink it on up my friends,
This life is a cup,
The best fillin' is free.

Sometimes when I'm about to pout,

I try to find a lighter route,

And give it a little time

To work itself on out.

Sometimes when I'm about to pout,

I try to find a lighter route,

And give it a little time

To work itself on out.

Sometimes when I'm about to pout,

I try to find a lighter route,

And give it a little time

To work itself on out.

Sometimes when I'm about to pout,

I try to find a lighter route,

And give it a little time

To work itself on out.

Bein' It

Lookin' through my pocket,

For my lighter, found my wallet.

Fumblin' 'round some more,

Some loose change, but still no score.

Starin' up above, for an answer from a dove,

I was givin' up my hope, when it hits me like a dope,

Lost then found, amazing grace,

And it brightens up my face.

Lost then found, amazing grace,

And it brightens up my face.

I was lookin' for a light, instead of bein' it.

Findin' a fight, instead o' freein' it.

Unstruck sound beatin' in my chest

226

Howls like the wind as I pass the test.
I was lookin' for a light, instead of bein' it.
Findin' a fight, instead o' freein' it.
Unstruck sound beatin' in my chest
Howls like the wind as I pass the test.
Aoooooooh
Aoooooooh.

Lookin' for that somethin'
To complete my own contentment
Is the greatest of illusions
If my heart's bypassed in fusion,
So I mock the mage's ruse,
So my soul's sure not to lose.
I may wander on my way,
But my conscience never strays.
Higher ground is just a place
In consciousness' face.
Higher ground is just a place
In consciousness' face.

I was lookin' for a light, instead of bein' it.
Findin' a fight, instead o' freein' it.
Unstruck sound beatin' in my chest
Howls like the wind as I pass the test.
I was lookin' for a light, instead of bein' it.
Findin' a fight, instead o' freein' it.
Unstruck sound beatin' in my chest
Howls like the wind as I pass the test.
Aoooooooh
Aoooooooh.
Aoooooooh
Aoooooooh.
Aoooooooh
Aoooooooh.

Points About Points

With a Point:

Nature of Smallest Scale Universals

A Philosophy of Science paper by

Nicholas David Mirisola

First Published in Volume X, Issue XII of

The International Journal of Research and Scientific Innovation

January 5, 2024

Abstract

This paper is an investigation of different aspects of the smallest scales possible and their relationships with larger-scale phenomena. The relationships between the abstract and the concrete aspects of philosophical perspectives about time and space are considered. The phenomenon of continuity of motion is discussed, and the small-scale philosophical implications of continuity of motion could help to explain the reasoning behind why the speed of light is the way that it is and why the speed of light squared is a constant. Fractions of a point are proven to be a useful idea to an extent, and a thought experiment that demonstrates speeds of fractions of a point per instant is included in this paper. Possible paradoxes related to singularities are discussed briefly within this paper, too. Absolute, relative, and unpredictable definitions of points and instants are discussed and shown to potentially provide some natural reasoning to observed discrepancies between scientific theories, perceived warping of space-time, and the uncertainty principle. Also, a philosophical interpretation of the term extra dimensions, which involves the idea of fractions of a point, could be useful for attempts at a unified theory of science and is included in this paper.

Nature of Smallest Scale Universals

The nature of the smallest scales theoretically possible can have large-scale ramifications when the large scale is considered as the philosophical sum of its parts. When considered cumulatively, the nature of the smallest scales can really add up to some significant larger scale repercussions. Even in the mystery of how something could exist instead of nothing, something existing at all is made more feasible by the realization that it is only asking the smallest possible amount, or an infinitesimal amount, or a mathematically approximately equal amount for the smallest scales to manifest as a phenomenon. This means that in one light, it's only asking for a large amount of approximately nothing for a everything to manifest. That sounds approximately like more reasoning behind how something could exist at all than just not knowing. It also parallels the vast amount of physical emptiness which science has revealed our Universe to be composed of. The nature of the smallest scales has other philosophical insights to offer as well. This paper aims to investigate the philosophical nature of the smallest scales, some of the small and large-scale relationships that are implicated by those philosophies, and some of the different repercussions that are the results of the philosophies involved.

Standard, Integer-Based

Continuity of Motion

Continuity of motion or movement at the smallest scales has several implications. As opposed to something like teleporting, where there are gaps of space between point A and point B that are not traversed through or accounted for, to move or be motion with continuity will be defined in this paper as traveling through each consecutive spatial amount that makes up the line between point A and point B successively. The term *standard* continuity of movement or motion will be used to describe continuity of motion or movement that does not reference any special, unusual, or partially inexplicable types of continuity like teleporting or super-positioning. The term integer-based movement will, in this paper, refer to a movement that is described using integer-based amounts of points per instant. The fastest speed that movement with standard, integer-based continuity could happen at on the smallest scales would be 1 of the smallest definable areas, or an infinitesimal amount of space, or 1 point per instant. This is because a greater rate of speed, like even 2 of the smallest definable or infinitesimal amounts of space, or points per instant, would either be like teleporting, not accounting for all of the space being traveled in some way or would otherwise not exhibit what has been referred to as standard continuity of movement. One infinitesimal, point-like amount of space per instant would also be the slowest speed at movement with standard, integer-based continuity. This is because slower speeds would involve amounts of space less than a point in value, which are either zero or describing fractions of a point in some light, and what is being defined as *integer-based continuity of movement* is, by definition, a phenomenon that involves amounts of space and time that are integers, such as one point and one instant. The rate of one point per instant would also, for continuous movement with standard, integer-based continuity, be a constant since there are no other rates at which it could be happening. This is arrived at via the process of elimination since the constraints of traveling at a rate slow enough to not be teleporting and still traveling fast enough to be moving in integer-based amounts greater than zero restrict the possible speeds that it could be happening at. This information could help to explain why there is a speed of light that is both a constant and a functional speed limit.

Besides being a very intuitive speed for movement to happen on the smallest scales, 1 point per instant would also be an example of naturally occurring reasoning for a scientific constant that is the speed limit for a type of phenomenon. This is fundamentally important because the implications of nature having good reasoning behind the way that it behaves are vast and much more logical than having to work with unknown reasoning behind naturally occurring constants and laws. There are several reasons why working with scales so small could force us to use logic to find the larger scale implementations of the one point per instant speed. The quantities are so small that they could require an infinite amount of sensitivity of any instrument or method used to measure them, which may not be attainable. Secondly, even if we could measure things that small, the act of measuring would surely change the result. This means that out of necessity, logic may have to play a primary role in determining what larger-scale phenomenon correlates to the one-point-per-instant speed limit constant that logic has provided and could be the only reliable method we have for putting the pieces together.

The Speed of Light's Correlation with the Speed of Standard, Integer-Based Continuity

When looking in nature for the speed that would correlate with this one infinitesimal amount of space, or point, per instant speed, the speed of light is the prime suspect. Not only is it a functional speed limit and a constant in some light, but the speed of light is also associated with all known atoms in chemistry and is the speed at which all known phenomena in the electromagnetic spectrum occur. Another key point is that it is also a constant in relation to matter and energy specifically, and continuity of motion has to do with that relationship to an extent. When looked at on the infinite scales, the speed of light, as fast as it may be, is still

231

proportionally approximately equal to zero in comparison to infinity. This is in tune with the idea of movement with continuity happening in an infinitesimal, one point-like amount per instant, which is also in one light mathematically approximately, but not exactly equal to zero in terms of the amounts of time and space.

The speed of sound can be ruled out as the larger scale correlation of the one point per instant on philosophical grounds. First of all, it is not the greatest speed that we know of that large-scale objects can move with standard continuity. Secondly, there is no sound at all in a vacuum where the speed of light is constant, which would be expected of it, and faster than the speed of sound. Third of all, the type of continuity that we are looking for in a constant is more generalized and should not be strictly dependent on interactions between multiple objects as much as the way that sound is. This leaves us with the speed of light to meet the criteria of being a naturally occurring speed limit and constant for movement with standard continuity described by the 1 point per instant logic.

It is unlikely that the speed of light is not the constant that matches the 1 point per instant speed of movement with standard, integer-based continuity because both describe a concordant speed limit for the same type of natural phenomenon that is a constant. It would add unnecessary complexity to the issue of deciphering the large-scale equivalent of the 1 point per instant speed if the candidate that fit the bill was assumed to be just a possibility. It is at least more rational to think that it is not a coincidence that there is mutual logical harmony in the description of movement with standard, integer-based continuity and the role that the speed of light plays in nature, and therefore, they are correlated.

Concreteness and Abstractness of Space and Time Perspectives

If the speed of light does correlate with the speed of movement with regular, standard, integer-based continuity, then there is the issue of what is happening with all of the movement that we see around us that happens at speeds slower than that to resolve. One center of this discussion is the notion of a point, an infinitesimal amount of space, or the smallest possible unit of space, depending on how it is defined. In one light, a point is so small by definition that it can be referred to as one-dimensional, meaning that we are referring to only one precise dimension of space, a normally three-dimensional entity. This is as concrete as we can be about what it means to be a point, but it is still an abstraction to some extent since referring to only one dimension of a three-dimensional thing is an abstract thing to do to an extent. It surely correlates conceptually to what we mean it to, but to talk about space, which is three-dimensional and logically a continuum as a strictly one-dimensional thing to an extent, is an abstracted frame of reference. If space is viewed as a continuum that you can zoom in on infinitely and, therefore, infinitely divisible, then the notion of a point may be approximately correct in some light but still subject to some philosophical limitations.

In one light, time is treated more abstractly the more we view it as the sum of its parts and is treated most concretely when it is related to the instant we refer to as the now. Instead of something like space that is most concretely viewed as three-dimensional being abstracted as being composed of abstracted one-dimensional objects, the opposite is the case with time, being most concretely viewed in terms of its one-dimensional instants and being abstracted to an extent when we refer to it as having three dimensions of past, present, and future. This is because we only ever can definitively observe one instant at a time, the now, and to speak of past, present, and future dimensions of time is to abstractly construct a continuum to an extent. We never actually witness a past, present, or future that is not to an extent describable as an abstract representation of the things happening in the most concrete amount of time we can observe, which is the instant known as the now. It is not to say that we cannot describe theoretical past, present, and future dimensions of time, do so with the use of infinitely divisible continuum logic, or do so with a degree of somewhat solid accuracy, but more to say that the more that we consider time to be three-dimensional, the more we have done so with abstractions. This entails that there may be discrepancies in the way that time is treated when abstracted like that as a result of the lens of our abstraction, just as there may be for space when we abstract one-dimensional aspects of a more concretely three-dimensional thing.

It is not to imply that our abstractions, which are based on concrete ideas, would not be expected to correlate with reality in either case. There is still something logical about the abstractions of one-dimensional points of space and time with three dimensions of past, present, and future. It is more to suggest that in order to be as objective as we can when dealing with abstractions, the differences between the abstractions and the concrete should be accounted for and accommodated by the abstractions in as concrete a way as possible if we want our abstractions to be as accurate as possible representations of the phenomena. This has some serious ramifications in the cases of space and time.

In the case of time, if one would like to be as objective as possible, it would most definitively be described in terms of instants since that is the most concrete amount we have ever witnessed. We know for sure that an instant exists because we are experiencing it right now. If we are going to extrapolate additional dimensions of it, since we know that it comes in amounts of one instant called the now from experience, constructing the abstraction of a sequence of instants would be the more objective way that we can do that, as opposed to treating it just like a continuum and not instant-based. If one would like to treat time like an infinitely divisible continuum, that is a theory to the extent that would only really work completely accurately if it factored in that its infinitesimal, or smallest units come in a size that is at least in some light constant, known as instants. Instants can be relatively defined, too, though, since three-dimensional time as a continuum is infinitely divisible, and you could define an instant as a relative relationship derived by dividing a portion of three-dimensional time by infinity, representing infinite parts and divisibility. That type of methodology somewhat preserves the notion of an instant while factoring in the relative nature of defining quantifiable increments of a continuum. This type of reasoning could shed some light on why time is only allotted one dimension instead of three, even in relativity theory. Another example of why instants are in some way concrete is the fact that we all know exactly what is meant by an instant, with a degree of complete precision. We could not know what we were talking about with a complete degree of precision if there was nothing to it. An instant is also logically the only amount of time that can happen at once, which entails that if time is happening, an instant is happening.

This means that to treat time like a continuum, which is still to some extent a logical thing to do, to be philosophically appropriate about the fact that an abstraction is being applied, one should limit, to some extent, the quantification of time to increments of instants, in order to preserve that which is concrete about the abstraction's logic. The fact that abstractions of multiple dimensions of time should be accommodating of the smallest units to an extent is because the smallest, infinitesimal units (one instant out of an infinite amount of a theoretical infinitely divisible time continuum) are the more physical part of the abstraction in some sense. This is backed by the fact that if you cannot use an instant or instants, known as a now, to describe something that happens in time in some way, you can't be describing something that happened in time at all since every type of thing that happens that is time-related has to do with an instant known as the now in some way, shape or form. This does not completely eliminate the notion of time as a continuum. In fact, referring to time as a continuum can be an objectively useful tool to an extent since it now manifests seamlessly and fluidly from one moment to the next in one sense. Since you could relate to time as a continuum composed of an infinite amount of theoretical instants known as the now, that means that, in a sense, three-dimensional time is still referred to as an infinitely divisible instant known as the now. Referring to time in terms of instants restricts it to the most universally physical possible interpretations. It implies that where the continuum and instant logic may be dissonant, the resolution should reflect the concreteness and abstractness appropriately. This means that any continuum-based time representations should be able to describe what is happening in each instant of the proposed time and that they now should be accounted for in some way, shape, or form for all proposed times to be objectively accurate. In one light, there is only one instant, the now, and 3-dimensional time is a perception-based construct, but it could be implied that in another light, we always see a continuum-style series of instants, and therefore, an instant is meaningless in and of itself and time is still somewhat infinitely divisible. Therefore, both concepts are useful, but to combine the two completely accurately, logical accommodations must be made when dealing with abstractions that factor in the logical limitations and parameters of the abstractions if one would like to be more concrete about it.

In the case of space, the inverse is true, and the infinitesimal, or *smallest units* or one-dimensional points are the more abstracted and theoretical. They could accommodate the larger, more concrete notion of space as a whole three-dimensional continuum in order to have the more abstract notions be in tune with the physical reality. This means that while theories about one dimension of space can still be logical to an extent and even approximately accurate, some accommodation of space as more holistic than that is required to produce the most completely concretely accurate abstraction. Space would be more concretely defined as a collection of parts than just a one-dimensional point and most concretely defined as a continuum since its one-dimensional parts are, in part, abstractions of limited perspective. Not only is a one-dimensional point an abstraction to an extent, but in addition to that, you could logically zoom in infinitely on any possible three-dimensional space, which logically proves that space is concretely defined as a continuum and infinitely divisible and not as indivisible parts. That proves that space's continuum nature is more concrete and that the nature of points is more abstract because if you can theoretically zoom in infinitely, then any quantifiable quantity, even if it is trying to be by definition as small as possible, is still not a hundred percent as small as possible because you could still zoom in on it or divide it further. Since a one-dimensional point is an integer-based abstraction of a more objectively described 3-dimensional continuum, in order for the abstraction of points to function as realistically as possible, some philosophical accommodations must be made about the point system so that it is in tune with the physicality of space as a 3-dimensional continuum if one is trying to refer to space objectively, or to its physical aspects. The point system, being more theoretical in nature, should be the part that compromises to accommodate for the physical nature of the continuum aspects to achieve that type of result.

This is not to say that points are not a useful tool or that a one-dimensional point as an idea does not correlate in some way, shape, or form with reality. If we are referring to an area of space that is a square, we can talk about the corner of the square and the point that defines it, and without this point-based logic, it is impossible to speak with precision about what we are defining, and it could be impossible for nature to manifest the phenomenon without using points. Even if space is most concretely viewed as an infinitely divisible continuum, that theory still leaves room for the infinite amount of precision that is part of the point-based logic, by definition of being infinitely divisible and infinite precision. It is more that if one would like to refer to an infinitely precise portion of an infinitely divisible continuum as concretely as possible, a compromise is required to factor in both types of logic.

It should be noted that the more concrete aspects of time and space are not necessarily the more correct aspects of them. That would only be true in the case that space and time are concrete phenomena. There is enough scientific evidence out there that defines space and time in ways that are not completely concrete to bring into question dealing with them in the most concrete ways since that might not be a completely accurate way to deal with something that is not concrete, has non-concrete aspects to it, or in some other light is influenced by abstract factors. There very well could be more truth in the more abstract lights and approaches available to deal with space and time, and there is nothing other than the intuitiveness of objective definitions to predict that space and time are actually physically definable in every way. Therefore, an objective definition may be more physically natural than what the abstractions have to offer. However, if space and time are not in every light solid phenomenon, the concrete definitions could be expected to be limited, not the whole story, and in some light flawed. To deal with the more abstract definitions of time, it could be that accommodations should be made in some sense by the physical definitions such that the abstract definitions are factored inappropriately.

If time and space are realistically approachable in non-physical ways, then we could expect to see some abstract correlations to natural phenomena occurring. The nature of space may very realistically have to deal with the more abstract nature of points as strictly one-dimensional somehow, and that may be in not concrete ways to some extent. Time as an infinitely divisible continuum may also have to be dealt with in more abstract and less concrete ways in order to be realistic about a more abstract and less concrete entity. In order to factor in both the concreteness and abstract natures of space and time, both methodologies may have to be compromised. It is also feasible that one could expect to achieve different results from different approaches, especially if the natures of time and space are naturally able to manifest in different ways, be approached in different ways, or be perceived in differing ways. Nature itself could very well have to deal with the same paradox that we are philosophically faced with and could be expected to behave paradoxically as a result. Fractal space and time, or a unified fractal space-time continuum could be a philosophically, logically, and mathematically legitimate natural phenomenon which resolves all of the paradoxes in question.

Fractions of a Point

There is a way to accommodate the continuum nature of space within the construct of the abstraction of points. It may seem like splitting hairs, but since three-dimensional space is most concretely described as a continuum, splitting hairs may be required of the abstraction to be in tune with the concrete continuum aspects of space and to compensate for the logical bias inherent in trying to divide something that is most concretely a continuum into the smallest possible, integer-based parts. What this paper will philosophically suggest, and philosophically prove to an extent, is that fractions of a point of space are a valid idea and tool to use. Fractions of a point are the compensation for the abstraction of points methodology to factor in the objectivity of space as a continuum while still preserving the abstraction of points to the greatest extent philosophically grounded to do so. If fractions of a point are used in conjunction with the point system, then the resulting theory represents a synthesis of part-based and continuum-based logics that is weighted appropriately to factor in that space's continuum nature is concretely relevant and that its point nature is, to an extent, an abstraction. The theory is an adjustment based on the fact that points, while still a useful concept, should accommodate the continuum logic.

The following is mathematical proof of the utility of fractions of a point. The conceptual validity of the use of fractions of a point will be proven by constructing a triangle at extremely small scales. Start with a straight, vertical line, that is, for the purpose of defining something, 10 points long. At the top of the line, add one point perpendicularly to the right of the top point, right next to it, such that now we have two sides of a triangle, a 90-degree angle, one complete corner, and two unfinished corners of a triangle. Now, if we connect the point we just added to the right of the top of the vertical line with the bottom point of the vertical line to form the new line that is the hypotenuse of our triangle, you may notice some very interesting results. The points toward the bottom of the hypotenuse are a fraction of a point away from the original straight, vertical line. Since the triangle gets thinner as it goes down and the top point of the hypotenuse starts at one point to the right of the original vertical line, the points being referenced are a distance of more than zero points away from the original vertical line since they are not the same as the original vertical line, and less than one point away from the original vertical line since it the triangle gets thinner as it goes down and started at a distance of 1 point to the right of the original vertical line. This is logical proof that they are fractions of a point and are a useful description of quantities of space.

The implications of this somewhat strange type of math may seem small in one light, to say the least, but can be quite profound when considered cumulatively. While individually, the sizes in question are fractions of an infinitesimal amount, which is already approximately, but not exactly equal to zero, if the whole is at all even theoretically describable as the sum of its parts, even if that is just to an extent, the implications of this type of math and logic can be expected to add up to a noticeable sum. There are at least some, probably a myriad, and quite possibly countless possible ways that measurements of space could be most accurately defined by fractions of a point, and therefore, at least some, probably a myriad, and possibly infinite ways that these types of measurements can pervade science and life. If one factors in chaos theory and the butterfly effect, even one fraction of a point measurement could theoretically have a large-scale, noticeable effect on a complex system.

Fractions of a Point Per Instant

These types of measurements and logic could be the explanation for the range of speeds happening below the one point per instant speed of a standard, integer-based continuity of movement or the speed of light. If fractions of a point are values that get factored into the physics of movement, which is a distinct possibility, then speeds like .5 points per instant are possible. If nature has to deal with irrational numbers like pi, rational numbers with repeating decimal activity, or even just the infinitesimal amounts of space with a value of .000…1, it is safe philosophically to deduce that a continuum with infinite divisibility and precision is required to accurately relate to those levels of mathematical precision. A fractal space-time continuum could mathematically encrypt fractions of a point information within itself in a self-similar, infinitely divisible manner. Since there are many plausible ways that fractions of a point values can pervade the math and science of the smallest scales, there are, therefore, many speeds that are fractions of a point per instant that are plausible and potentially even likely to be expectable. This doesn't mean that points need to be thrown to the wayside, but rather that if points are in use, their divisibility is a compromise that must be factored in to adjust for the fact that it is to some extent untenable to simply divide an entity like space with a continuum nature into integer-based, quantifiable parts, even if the parts are by one definition as small as quantifiable parts can be.

It may be noteworthy to mention that there are other possible solutions to what is happening with all of the speeds we observe that are not happening at the suspected speed of light's rate. However, they are not necessarily as philosophically sound as the portions of a point logic and don't necessarily come with the same type of proof, either. Two of them have to do with the notion of a point as being the smallest, indivisible possible increment of space and base their logic around that. Neither one is a completely viable retort to the mathematical proof of fractions of a point, however. Both avoid the use of fractions of a point to at least an extent, which could be a partial mistake in light of the logic used about the physicality of space as a continuum and the fact that a point is at least to some extent a theory and therefore distanced philosophically from what is objective about space. For the purpose of covering the bases philosophically and because it may be impossible to completely disprove them, this paper will discuss them both.

The Strictly Integer-Based Motion Methodology

If one ascribes to the notion of a point as being as small as possible, with no further division possible, it would appear that 1 point per instant would be the only speed at which movement with standard continuity could happen. It should be noted that a point as indivisibly small is a man-made construct to an extent and could be flawed to an extent as an abstraction in and of itself. One point per instant would be the only speed that integer-based, standard continuity could happen at because increments of space would be dealt with in integer-based amounts, so 1 point per instant would be the slowest, fastest, and constant speed that movement with standard continuity could happen at. If it was happening any slower, the next integer-based value below one point per instant would be zero points per instant, which would not be movement or motion at all. If it was happening at a rate greater than 1 point per instant, it could be perceived as teleporting or not accounting for all of the space traveled in what has been defined as a strictly standard way since it is at least not necessarily logically clear what it would mean to be traveling at a rate greater than 1 point per instant for a point sized object. If you ascribe strictly to the notion of all movement or motion happening at the rate of one point per instant because points are as small as possible in one light, then there is a convoluted explanation available for speeds slower than that.

The first type of explanation for the case where there was only movement and/or motion happening with standard, integer-based continuity, all at a constant rate of one point per instant, without any stopping and starting or slowing down and speeding up. In this methodology, things are either moving at a rate of one point per instant or completely still. In this version of a response to why we seem to observe speeds slower than the speed of light or the one point per instant speed, on larger than infinitesimal scales, things could appear to be moving with continuity from large-scale observable point A to point B. This would appear to happen at speeds slower than the one infinitesimal unit of space per instant speed or the speed of light, but actually be an illusion. The illusion could be similar to using red and yellow pixels that are too small to see individually and produce the larger-scale observable phenomenon of seeing the color orange instead of just red and yellow. Or it could be analogous to perceiving a motion video as fluid, when in actuality it is a rapid sequence of discretely different individual frames. It would not be the first of nature's illusions, like the flat Earth or the illusion of standing still, when in fact the Earth is spherical and rotating at speeds around 1000 miles per hour at the equator, while it revolves around the sun at speeds around 67,000 miles per hour. The illusion could work something like this. Because the microscopic movement of the points in orbits or other circuitous paths is too small to be measured, they could theoretically still be traveling at a rate of one point per instant microscopically. At the same time, they simultaneously seem to traverse from point A to point B of a larger observable scale at a slower rate by producing an illusion. This could result in movement that appears at larger scales to be happening continuously in one direction but is actually a composite of microscopic subatomic orbital paths that backtrack and do not travel in a straight line from point A to point B. For example, a tiny object could make a small amount of progress from large-scale observable point A to point B every revolution. A revolution could take one second, and it could overall make one inch of lateral progress. So, it would seem to the larger scale that it is moving at a rate of one inch per second, which is slower than the speed of light. The overall speed of progress from larger scale observable point A to point B could seem like it was happening slower than the speed of light or the speed of a standard, integer-based continuity of motion, even though all of the microscopic movements of the object that were too small to be measured by the larger scale instruments was happening at the speed of one infinitesimal amount of space per instant, or the speed of light continuously for the duration of the second that it took to perform the revolution and register as a lower than light speed rate of movement per second. This could be one explanation for the resulting illusion of speeds on larger scales that do not seem to be happening at the speed limit while leaving the integer-based point-like amount of space per instant speed of movement with the continuity rule strictly intact.

This version, while potentially impossible to disprove completely, relies on the assumption that all of the movement we see that is not happening at the speed of one point per instant is an illusion, which is, at the least, asking a lot philosophically. While it is simple in terms of its treatment of points as the indivisibly smallest units of space, that costs it the added complexity of assuming that observable science is an illusion to some extent. This method also denies and tries to refute the validity of known scientific measurements of speed as an illusion, which is contrary to the body of evidence that we have to work with. It also does not deal with fractions of a point, which could have at least some mathematically valid contributions to make. Therefore, it could be approximately correct in one light but may not be a completely precise representation of reality in spite of that. It is an approach that seems to be, by design, avoiding the use of fractions of a point. Since fractions of a point have at least some mathematical and logical proof behind their use, this particular approach can be at least limited, probably not the whole story, and at most flawed.

Staggered Continuity of Motion

The second alternate method of dealing with speeds that are slower than the one point per instant speed would involve what this paper will refer to as staggered continuity of movement or motion. This type of movement would involve moving one point per multiple instants of time. This type of motion would entail moving one point in a given direction only one out of the multiple instants and being somehow stationary for the duration of the rest of the multiple instants. For example, an object could move at a rate of 1 point per 3 instants, which would translate to it moving once at a rate of one point per instant for one instant and being stationary for the remaining two instants, then possibly repeating this pattern. If this is even a plausible method in some light, then there is the issue of the mechanisms of how that is dealt with, which may or may not be resolvable to a satisfactory extent if the method is considered in isolation. While one interpretation of this method could preserve the notion of points as the smallest indivisible units and still adhere to the one point per instant speed as the only speed thing can happen to an extent like the last method described, it would also, like the last method, require the assumption that all of the observable evidence we have of speeds slower than the speed of light or the speed of integer-based standard continuity of movement is an illusion in a similar way and that observable science has been duped by nature to an extent, which is not necessarily a sound argument in some lights.

How is the information about how that is happening in this method preserved and mechanistically put into action? A quantum mechanics type of explanation could be that it is making a quantum leap of one point every three instants, but that still leaves the classical physicists' perspectives unsatisfied to an extent. A classical physics-related explanation for the conservation of the information of energy could be that the point in question is laterally stationary but spinning and that somehow it translates that motion into lateral movement of one point every three instants. However, the stop-and-go motion of the point in question still is not necessarily completely resolved in a more classical sense. Also, if you are going to ascribe to the notion of spinning points, then how exactly does that manifest without using fractions of a point as measurements in at least some sense? It could be explained to an extent with what this paper will refer to as self-referencing continuity of rotational motion, which will be discussed later in the paper. This alternative method of dealing with speeds slower than one point per instant by assigning a speed of one point per multiple instants does try to provide a methodology that explains such phenomena. However, the explanation lacks a completely coherent mechanistic approach in some light for how that happens, supposes that the evidence we have collected is an illusion, and avoids dealing with fractions of a point. That means that this approach is also at least limited, probably not the whole story, and at most flawed.

Continuity of Rotational Motion

Further investigation of the notion of spin in relation to points will reveal some insight. If a point has spin, then it is either spinning at a rate of one absolutely defined infinitesimal amount of a degree per instant to have a semblance of absolutely defined continuity of movement, some amount of relatively defined degrees greater than that but less than a full rotation per instant to have what this paper will refer to as relative continuity of movement or motion, or a full spin per instant and exhibit what this paper will refer to as self-referencing continuity.

Absolutely Defined Continuity of Rotational Motion

Absolutely defined continuity, in this case, refers to the aspect of the motion of a spinning point, or anything spinning, for that matter, which is a reflection of the fact that it is rotating such that it consecutively cycles through the possible positions in a successive manner, based on an absolute type of definition of the smallest possible amount of rotation, or an absolute infinitesimal amount of a degree, or .000...1 degree. For example, first, it would rotate one infinitesimal amount of a degree, or .000...1 degree, then it would continue to rotate similarly, though it should be noted that just like the point per instant speed, fractions of a unit could be necessary to fully cover the continuum nature of space in this description. The absolute type of definition of an infinitesimal amount of a degree would be a universally relevant and standardized measurement, to an extent, based on dividing 360 degrees of infinite theoretical space into infinite parts. There may be ways of rotating an object that produces increments that are fractions of a point different from the absolute type of definition described, however.

Relative Continuity of Motion and A Thought Experiment Exhibiting Fractions of a Point Per Second

A fairly simple thought experiment can demonstrate both the term relative continuity and give an example of something traveling at a rate of fractions of a point per instant. If there is a vertical line that is 10 points long, and it is rotating such that the bottom point remains fixed like a pivot point that is the center of a circle, the top point is moving at a rate of one point per instant, and the line remains fairly straight throughout the process, then this example illustrates both of the aforementioned concepts. First of all, the points near the somewhat anchored bottom of the line will be moving at a rate of a fraction of a point per second since some of the same type of logic that was involved in the first triangle mathematical proof is involved, but this time as a progression in time. If the top of the line moves at a rate of one point per instant, the bottom point is anchored in place, and the line remains somewhat straight. The points toward the bottom of the line will travel a distance of less than one point in the same instant. It takes the top of the line to move one point, which would be a fraction of a point per instant. This is mathematical and logical proof of concept to an extent, and the basic premise should also hold true enough of larger objects to get the point across, even if the premise of a line-based thought experiment is limited, on shaky grounds, or flawed scientifically. With an adjustment, it will also demonstrate what is meant by relative continuity of motion.

If the length of the rotating line stretched upward to infinity and moved one infinitesimal amount of a degree, then the point at the bottom of the line would rotate in the manner previously defined as having absolute continuity of rotational motion, rotating one absolutely defined type of infinitesimal amount of a degree per instant. For practical purposes, we don't have infinite lines to work with in everyday life that we know of other than as abstractions, and to some extent, nature may not either, so a different methodology will be used to rotate smaller length lines the smallest possible practical distance. This will result in the number of degrees of rotation being based on the idea of moving the top point of the line one point each time and would result in differences of fractions of a point in the values produced, and could be a more practically applicable method in some ways of defining rotation than the use of absolutely defined infinitesimal amounts of a degree.

The top end of the shorter-than-infinite lines will be moved one point at a rate of one point per instant such that the line rotates around the bottom point just like before since that may be in one light be a more common application of the concepts. The shorter we make the rotating line, the more the points toward the bottom of the line move at a greater rate of speed, still fractions of a point per instant, but all values greater than if we moved the theoretically infinite line as small an amount as possible. It can be noticed that if this methodology is used to rotate something, then the amount of rotation of the points below the top is relative to the length of the line. This is what was meant by relative continuity of rotational movement. While it may not have the absoluteness of value that a standardized infinitesimal amount of a degree could have if you could rotate an infinite line by one point, it may still prove to be an important concept because of its practicality and how common it could be.

Self-Referencing Continuity of Rotational Motion

The third type of continuity left to be defined was the self-referencing, or self-similar, continuity of rotational movement. This type of rotation could only describe points referencing themselves as one-dimensional and rotating to some extent. This is because the more absolute or standardized regular continuity of rotational motion describes rotational motion in reference to infinite theoretical space, relative continuity of rotational motion describes continuity of the type smaller than infinitely-based but bigger than a point in scope to some extent, and what is left is to define if a point rotates in reference to just itself. Since a point is theoretically so small that it is one-dimensional in one light, which is like saying it is completely small, which is also like saying that it is all edge, to rotate for something one-dimensional has the theoretical capability of meaning a full rotation in one instant. This is because it is only one dimensional, and while rotation may have to do with two or three dimensions normally, any amount of rotation of just one point in reference to just itself could be considered equivalent to a full rotation since it is not bounded by two or three-dimensional constraints, and just in relation to itself, it can be considered to just have a one-dimensional area. How could the two-dimensional constraint of having to rotate a certain amount of two-dimensional degrees be translated into a one-dimensional self-referencing object? Since it is small enough to be a one-dimensional point, then any amount of strictly one-dimensional rotation would be an amount great enough to rotate it. A full rotation is a logical premise, which is logically achieved by referencing itself as only one-dimensional and disregarding a two or three-dimensional context to an extent. It would only be achievable in relation to just itself as a one-dimensional object to some extent because if you factored in two or three dimensions as frames of reference with relationships with the one-dimensional point, it could be discredited to at least an extent.

This particular type of motion is certainly abstract and possibly an abstraction at best, and with space being a three-dimensional entity, it may be mostly irrelevant or refutable. Nevertheless, it may play a role in singularities, particularly if there is a singularity at the beginning of the Big Bang that had an infinite temperature, as has been speculated. If a singularity was infinitely divisible by fractions of a point in the relationship with a three-dimensional context but was rotating in the self-referencing way described because it was the only one-dimensional area of space defined by the speculated singularity, that could help to explain how seemingly competing values of infinite temperature and a single point could be more harmoniously co-existent. There could be infinite fractions of a point repercussions as soon as it expanded and was translated into a three-dimensional context. If centripetal force applies to point-sized scales in fractions of point ways, then that could even help to explain why it expanded in the first place. Also, the infinite divisibility of a point could help to explain the speculated infinite density of the big bang theory's associated speculated singularity. The Big Bang could have even been a fractal seed for the universe which necessitated its own existence philosophically in order for nature to resolve the paradox of abstractions versus physicality of the space-time continuum itself.

If self-referencing continuity of motion was used in the explanation of staggered continuity of motion, then there could be some explanation for how a point mechanistically achieves staggered continuity of movement. If sometimes the point was exhibiting self-referencing continuity of motion, then that could possibly translate into lateral movement. Similarly, maybe it could translate the lateral motion into self-referencing rotational motion. Since a full rotation in an instant would mean that it is somewhat paradoxically also in the same position that it started in within the same instant, it is possible that it could be subject to the interpretation that it is not moving at all, too. If both possibilities are options for different ways that self-referencing continuity of rotational motion could manifest, then there could be some semblance of a mechanistic explanation for the staggered continuity of motion discussed previously.

Relative Relationships and Continuity of Motion

Another way that speeds are slower than the speed of light or integer-based standard continuity of motion could be achieved involves the relative warping of space of the type that is comparable to use in the Theory of Relativity. If it is possible to warp space-time similar to the way that it is predicted by Relativity types of theory, then it is, to an extent, possible for those types of distortions to play a role in observing speeds slower than the speed of integer-based, standard continuity. If it is possible to calculate space and time relatively to some extent, which it is in some light, then point and instant values can be calculated relatively. While they could be conserved conceptually to an extent, the solutions would differ somewhat from the absolutely defined values of both.

Absolutely Defined Space and Time

If the size of a point and the duration of an instant are considered to be absolutely defined values only, then in that light, it is impossible for them to be warped. The warping of space and time would have to be an illusion in some light that can be described by the type of math that would accomplish warping space and time. Absolutely defined values could be arrived at by dividing infinity by infinity, representing infinite possible space and time and infinite possible parts, respectively, and would be somehow standardized units since that calculation would, in some way, provide mathematically constant, consistent results. The standardized units would be infinitesimals, which points and instants are, but would be uniform and homogenous because the same math would be used to calculate the size of every part. The results of those types of calculations could also be related to integer-based amounts of points and instants to an extent. This may sound like a strictly

244

classical physics type of approach. However, there could very well be something to it, if nothing more than the definition of absolutely defined points, infinitesimals, or the smallest possible units.

Relatively Defined Space and Time

If the size of a point and an instant is at all relative, however, then there is a way to explain the perceived warping of space-time. If you divide a cubic meter into infinite infinitesimal parts and 10 cubic meters into infinite infinitesimal parts, couldn't the size of the 10 cubic meter parts be relatively bigger than the size of the one cubic meter parts in one mathematical sense? This would be because you would be dividing a measurably bigger object by the same, constant amount of infinity in one sense. As an example, if we divided each by the same number, say 100, the 100 parts of the 10 cubic meters would be bigger than the 100 parts of the single cubic meter. Any division problem or fraction with a constant number as the denominator will produce smaller parts the smaller you make the numerator. If the size of infinitesimal areas of space is relative in this way, then it is possible to explain space as seeming to warp by being defined as relatively different-sized infinitesimals.

Maybe the differences in the sizes of the infinitesimals are fractions of a point, which could result in both being divisible by infinity but producing different results. If the notion of a point is relatively related to, instead of absolutely related to, then dividing by infinity to calculate point size would produce different values depending on the size of the measurement of the size that it is relative to. This would mean that larger areas' points, when considered relative to the area defined, would be larger, and any point-based calculations that are factored in this type of math would produce different results than smaller areas' point-based calculations in some light. Since points can be described in one light as infinitesimal, and space has a continuum type of nature to an extent, defining points as relative infinitesimal sizes could be a useful way of relating to how they can theoretically be applied. The same type of relative calculations could be used to calculate the duration of an instant of time, with larger amounts of time producing relatively larger infinitesimal parts when divided by a constant infinity.

The effects of these types of calculations could be analogous to the mathematical, philosophical, and possibly physical effect, appearance, or illusion of space or space-time warping, depending on how you interpret it. If you were speaking strictly relatively about space but still trying to adhere to the point per instant speed, or the speed of light as a constant the way that relativity does, then it is possible to say that the same constant concept of a point would be a smaller amount of space to traverse and therefore take a smaller amount of time to traverse on smaller relative scales where the points are relatively smaller than it would on larger scales. So, time could seem to happen faster relative to the constant point per instant speed at smaller relative scales. It would also, for the same number of points traveled, result in smaller amounts of space being traveled. This could produce a phenomenon in which space seemed smaller on relatively smaller scales. This would be logically coherent to an extent because the method of arriving at what it means to be a point is calculated relatively while still adhering to the notion of points to an extent, which means that points and instants are relatively preserved conceptually as constants, but relatively adjusted to the conditions. It would also at least somewhat preserve the logic behind why the speed of integer-based, standard continuity of motion is the way that it is and functions the way that it does, which it would have good philosophical reasons to do. The fact that points and instants are approachable as absolutely definable amounts could be the reason that the notion is somewhat preserved. The fact that that is not the only way to define them could result in some reasoning behind why other ways of calculating their values could be observed in nature. That could help shed some light on why the theory of relativity treats the speed of light as a constant, too.

Multiple Approaches to the Same Phenomenon

The fact that there are absolutely definable and relatively definable ways of relating to points that would both produce different results could help to explain why there are different classical physics types of explanations, which tend to treat space and time as absolute, and the Theory of Relativity types of explanations, which tend to treat space and time as relative. A similar type of multiple approaches logic could help to explain the differing potential applications of the theory of integer-based, standard continuity of motion. If nature itself has multiple ways to treat phenomena, then it is logical that we would find multiple scientific ways to treat phenomena, too. Therefore, it is logical to infer that, having found multiple scientific and philosophical ways to treat phenomena, one reason we could find different ways to approach phenomena is that nature itself has multiple ways to deal with phenomena.

The Uncertainty Principle of Quantum Mechanics

If nature genuinely has multiple ways of defining itself, then this could be good reasoning behind why we would expect to see Heisenberg's uncertainty principle in nature. If nature has multiple ways of processing the same information that would each produce different results, then why and how would it possibly manifest just one consistently? It is possible that nature is faced with the same issue of competing theories that we are. As a result of the nature of there being multiple solutions to the same problem, multiple solutions to the natural phenomena are factored in somehow. It is also possible that each possible solution is better at certain ways of dealing with phenomena and that the theory that is the best at dealing with a certain type of phenomenon is the one that is employed to an extent. It is also possible, however, that there are phenomena that are not necessarily better described by one theory or another, and the appropriate manifestation of the phenomena would not be clear. It could very well be that nature itself sometimes, if not potentially even always to some extent, doesn't have a good enough reason to manifest points in either a relative way or an absolute way. Therefore, there would be no reason good enough to expect complete predictability from such a system to an extent.

If there is no reason that hands down outweighs the significance of another reason for a phenomenon to manifest in a certain way, and predictability is therefore not expectable from a system to an extent, unpredictability to an extent could actually be what to predict from such a system. This unpredictability, to an extent, is exactly what we find in Heisenberg's uncertainty principle's relationship with quantum mechanics, which it would be expected to exhibit. The fact that it is just to an extent and that the more probable an event is to happen, the more it does happen could be a byproduct of the fact that there are certain things in common between the competing theories, which could produce trends in a not completely predictable environment that did have certain things in common between different possible manifestations.

If nature had different possible manifestations of a phenomenon depending on whether it calculated point size absolutely or relatively, the possible solutions would still have points and instants in common to an extent but still not be completely predictable to manifest as either the absolute form or the relative, so some semi-predictable, semi-unpredictable trends could be expected from the semi-predictable, semi-unpredictable nature of that phenomenon. There are a theoretically infinite number of ways of defining a point relatively because of the theoretically infinite amount of sub-divisions of the space continuum that could be used to calculate a point's relative size, as discussed earlier, and they would all produce a different result. Just one of them, the one that calculated a point or instant's size relative to all of infinite theoretical space or time, would produce the same type of point as the absolutely defined point. That would be something that they had in common. Even if you tried to calculate a point relatively in relation to infinite possible space, you would still get the same result that you got by calculating the absolute definition of a point because the math involved would be the same infinity divided by infinity type. Just having one solution in common might not seem like much, and in one light, it isn't much considering that there is an infinity minus one amount of differences. However, it does show that the two theories do relate somehow and is an example of using two methodologies to arrive at the same result. While each individual point's different definition could be relatively different by fractions of a point in an absolute sense, that means that nature could be presented with the option, in a sense, of defining a point in one absolute way or defining it in an infinite number of relative ways. That entails that even if absolute points are a more intuitive idea in a sense, the one absolutely defined point's possible manifestation is outnumbered infinity minus one to one by the number of possible relative definitions of a point as possible ways a point could manifest just relatively. Whether absolutely defined points and instants are a more intuitive idea or not, there are still an infinite amount of possible ways that nature could manifest the phenomena of points, infinitesimals, or the smallest units of space, and therefore, an infinite amount of unpredictability that could be expected to manifest naturally and philosophically alongside the constant notion of points which could provide some degree of predictability. This could help to explain why we can best describe a quantum event's probability of occurring, which is like saying that they are semi-predictable, semi-unpredictable in one light.

Defining a Point

If the decision between defining points relatively or absolutely did not seem like purely a good enough reason to expect uncertainty from nature to some extent, then the definition of how a point is defined and how that translates to two-dimensional and three-dimensional manifestations of the phenomena should provide enough philosophical, logical, and mathematical reason in some light. In defining a point, it should be noted that there are multiple angles to consider and that each one could produce different results, so once again, it would appear that nature may very realistically have some metaphorical options as to how it manifests itself.

A point, by definition, refers to a part of space that is one-dimensional or a reference to just one dimension of three-dimensional space. This is a very useful definition, and there is something to be said for the soundness of the logic used in this definition. It is saying that if you refer to a point, your perspective of space is so small that you are really referring to one dimension of a three-dimensional object. If you were to divide space infinitely, it makes sense that the answer you got would, to some extent, not be bound to be expressed in three dimensions since infinity is a boundlessly large amount, by definition. This means that there is some concurrent logic in describing points as infinitesimal amounts of space. Both would also be expected to be infinitesimal values. A definition of a point that may provide us with some more information as to how it translates to a three-dimensional setting could be that a point is the smallest possible unit of space in some light.

The definition of a point as strictly one-dimensional is its most absolute, concrete, and precisely defined definition. However, it is also an abstraction to the extent of the naturally three-dimensional space continuum, so its utility is limited to describing useful applications in relation to three-dimensional space. The definition of a point as an infinitesimal could shed more light on possible three-dimensional applications. While that may prove to be a more concrete way of defining a point in relation to a three-dimensional continuum, it is a more abstract way of defining a one-dimensional object. The definition of a point as an infinitesimal can be related to a compromise between the notion of a point as strictly one-dimensional and the definition of a point as the smallest possible quantifiable area. The definition of a point as the smallest possible unit of space, which can be related to ideas like area and volume, maybe the most concrete way to speak of how points are defined in and translated to a three-dimensional continuum setting. However, it is the most abstractly distanced way of referring to any concreteness that is involved in the logic of strictly one-dimensional points. Since it has been established that one-dimensional points are to some extent an abstraction and that space is, in some light, concretely a three-dimensional continuum as a phenomenon, methods that are a bit more abstractly distanced from the one-dimensional definition of a point and closer to three-dimensional continuum definitions of a point could prove to be more concrete ways of dealing with the notion of points to some extent.

How a point relates to a three-dimensional setting is critical because the concreteness of the definition of space as a three-dimensional continuum should be considered when dealing with the somewhat abstract notion of a point. Since it is not that there is nothing at all concrete about the logic of one-dimensional points, that logic should still play a role in determining how points most concretely translate into a three-dimensional setting. If points are defined as absolutely as possible by dividing infinite potential space, which would correlate to infinite points, by infinity, the solution is a concrete but potentially enigmatic 1 or one point. The number 1, in an absolute definition of points, would translate to a measurement of points as one-dimensional and could also be used as a measurement of area and volume. To do that in a way that is in accordance with points' definition as one-dimensional, you could interpret the value of one point as being a unit of one point one-dimensionally, a one-dimensional one-point unit of area, and a one-dimensional unit of one-point could be used as a unit to describe a point's volume, in an absolute sense. These absolutely defined points would be expected to be uniform and standardized since the math works out exactly the same every time, and there is, in an absolutely defined sense, only one possible definition for the dimensions of a point, which is limited to being one-dimensional. This also could serve as mathematical evidence of some concreteness of the notion of strictly one-dimensional, absolutely defined points. If it only has one dimension and all of the parts have the same one-dimensional description, the math works out the same for every one of those absolutely defined points. They are standardized and uniformly exactly one-dimensional points. This may seem like the most appropriate way to define points in one light. While this definition is an absolute type, it brings us no closer to describing how points relate to three-dimensional space because they are still being described in terms of a solely one-dimensional abstraction, and this is a biased abstraction of a somewhat concretely three-dimensional space continuum, which limits its relevance and usefulness. Therefore, while there may be some absoluteness, some usefulness, and some truth to that type of definition of a point, there is good reason to seek other explanations, methods, or compensations for this method's inherent abstraction biases.

If points are defined relatively by dividing non-infinite areas of space by infinity, then points would have the notion of themselves as points in common to an extent. There would be slight variations in their relative translation to two and three-dimensional settings. Because this definition would involve dividing smaller-than-infinity numerators by the constant of infinity, we could mathematically expect the results to be smaller as the numerator gets smaller and for all possible results calculated relatively to be smaller in some sense than the absolute value that is calculated with infinity as the numerator. While this type of definition does not have the same absoluteness as the last definition, it may be more appropriate in some senses because objects in nature do not necessarily come in infinite sizes.

Therefore, smaller than infinite size-based calculations could actually be a more common phenomenon than the absolute definition in some light. To an extent, a relative definition of points also evokes and requires more continuum-based logic to represent the points defined and involves defining each subsequent point in relation to a two or three-dimensional setting, even in defining their smallest dimension/s, which can be avoided by the absolute definition if you were to say that a point is simply one dimensional and that's the end of the story.

The Smallest Possible Scales, Infinitesimal-Based, Standard Continuity of Motion, and the Speed of Light Squared

If one were to try to define the smallest possible scale while trying to factor in points and instants as somewhat integer-based values, one would also factor in that both time and space can be described as continuum-based. Therefore, infinitely divisible as well, then there is some related math involved that could be important. If we represent the speed of one point per instant proportionally as $1/\infty$ amount of space per amount of time, since a point per instant is infinitesimal in value and it can be represented mathematically by the proportion one divided by infinity as a speed, then we can divide that number by infinity to factor in that even the infinitesimal values are divisible by infinity. Doing so would be philosophically and mathematically factoring in that they are infinitesimal values that are part of an infinitely divisible continuum instead of just assuming that the infinitesimal units of points as strictly integer-based are the smallest possible measurements in every light. Ascribing a value of $1/\infty$ amounts of space per amount of time would also factor in the integer-based aspects of points and instants mathematically with the use of the number one in the numerator, which implies that they can come in integer-based amounts to some extent. Dividing $(1/\infty)$ units of space per $(1/\infty)$ amount of time by infinity should be enough to infinitely mathematically and philosophically compensate for the idea of each space and time value as an integer-based value in an infinitely divisible, continuum-based interpretation. Dividing by an infinite amount of space per amount of time would factor in that even points' and instants' integer-based interpretations are parts of an infinitely divisible continuum.

$(1/\infty)/\infty$ is also equal to $(1/\infty) \times (1/\infty)$, which is also equal to $(1/\infty)2$, which would be equivalent to multiplying the point per instant speed by one point per instant or squaring the point per instant speed. Squaring the infinitesimal equivalent of the point per instant speed would be philosophically, logically, and mathematically equivalent to squaring the constant point per instant speed in some light since squaring the philosophical equivalent produces the desired interpretation's value and the two are philosophically logically, and mathematically equivalent in some way.

Since the concept of both space and time as continuum-based and integer-based are both constants and this type of math factor is in both, the point per instant squared value or the speed of light squared would be expected to be a mathematical constant, too. It would also help to represent the smallest possible amount of motion per the smallest possible amount of time possible. Therefore, it should be a constant describing continuity of motion or movement in an infinitesimal-based way, as opposed to a strictly integer-based way. This is because the way standard continuity of motion can happen with fractions of a point involved that describe time and space in terms of somewhat absolutely one-dimensional aspects of an infinitely divisible continuum would be in the smallest possible increments as they progress through each successive smallest possible continuum-based one-dimensional aspects, which would be described by the point per instant squared math and logic.

Because of how constant the notion of a strictly one-dimensional instant is and the fact that there is something logical about one-dimensional point logic, the point per instant squared value would be expected to be a mathematical and logical constant. It could be describing the motion of infinitesimal-based, standard continuity of motion, as opposed to integer-based, standard continuity of motion. It would be expected to be a philosophical constant because what it would mean to exhibit infinitesimal-based, standard continuity of motion would be logically based around the constants of movement with standard continuity that are based, this time, on infinitely divisible increments of points and instants that are standardized by the constant, absolute definitions of one-dimensional points and instants. Since the type of infinitesimal-based, standard continuity of motion or movement described by the point per instant squared logic could be expected to be a constant because of the philosophical conditions of what it means to exhibit continuity of motion or movement to some extent, the mathematical representation of a point per instant squared would also, being associated with the smallest possible scale philosophical constants, be to an extent a constant, which we do find scientifically, mathematically, and philosophically in nature.

Since we find in nature things moving at speeds that would correlate to integer-based, standard continuity of motion like the speed of light, speeds slower than that, and the speed of light squared as a constant describing matter's relationship with energy, which involves motion, and all three are describing different types of continuity of motion, it makes sense to deduce that different types of continuity of motion are possible in nature. Since some are integer-based, some are relatively based on fractions of a point, and some are based on points as infinitely divisible, it is logical to infer that nature can relate to points in all three ways to some extent, just like we can philosophically. That means that points are, in one light, a useful measurement in and of themselves, that they are divisible and partially relevant in some lights, and that they are infinitely divisible and therefore an abstraction in one light, and the same could be said of an infinite now in relation to the concept of instants. It is quite possible, then, that nature is presented with the same seemingly paradoxical attributes and that each type of description is somewhat unique but can still be related to in terms of the other explanations. That means that it is possible that points and instants are not necessarily just describable theoretically as integers, fractions, and infinitely divisible, but even definable as integers, fractions, and infinitely divisible constituents of a continuum which can be defined in terms of each other.

Defining Points as Three-Dimensional Limits

If points are described this time as points that are three-dimensional limits, then the absoluteness of their definition can be compromised to an extent, which, while it may cost losing some of the concreteness of an absolute definition, should bring us closer to relating it to the concreteness of space as a three-dimensional continuum. To fit the purpose of the type of philosophies involved, this paper will use a three-dimensional setting to try to help define points on an individual basis. Some basic logic can help us to realize how points can relate to a three-dimensional setting. First of all, if we use a more calculus type of methodology than invoking infinitesimals or describing points as simply having only one-dimensional relevance that doesn't translate into three-dimensions at all, and we approach the idea of a point as a calculus type of limit. There is some mathematical logic available to shed some light on the subject. If a point is viewed as a limit in three-dimensional space, then we should be able to do some calculations about how that limit is describable. Sounds simple, but has some complex repercussions.

First, we'll start with some logic to define the parameters of what is to be expected of how points relate to a three-dimensional environment. If we have a straight vertical line and take away one point in the middle of it, we can deduce that we are now left with two lines. This means that one valid interpretation or aspect of a point's nature is that a point has a height of one point in value. If we also have a line that runs horizontally and one that runs front to back, and we line them up such that they all intersect perpendicularly at the same point's location on the vertical line that was just discussed, we now have what looks like the x, y, and z axes of a standard graph. If we take away the point in the middle where they intersect, this time, we can deduce that we now have 6 lines instead of 3 because we subtracted the point of intersection. This means that we can logically infer that a point can relate to a three-dimensional context as being describable as having a height of one point, a width of one point, and a depth of one point because if that was not true, then we would not be left with 6 lines instead of 3. So, if we are looking at a point as a description of a limit in three-dimensional space, logic would insist that somehow it at least relates to three dimensions as having a width, depth, and height of one point.

What to do about this information could be more puzzling than at first glance could seem, however. If one were to calculate all of the possible shapes that could possibly manifest with a width, height, and depth of 1 point, several complications are encountered. First of all, none of the shapes that you can use to describe a point as a three-dimensional limit avoid invoking the use of fractions of a point in their description. If you were to relate to pieces of the three-dimensional shapes of any possible three-dimensional representation of a point that had a width, height, and depth of one point, you could definitely always find at least one way of dividing it that would require a mathematical description that utilized fractions of a point. This is because the additional geometric complexity inherent in a three-dimensional representation of a point provides an infinitely divisible sub-point context with which to measure. This could be more evidence that fractions of a point are a necessary tool in some light for point-based systems to compensate for the continuum aspects of space, and it doesn't necessarily have to mean that all of the options are completely flawed because of that.

Secondly, none of the possible shapes that could describe a point as a three-dimensional limit have a width, height, depth, area, and volume that all equal 1 point in some light unless you refer to the more absolute way of defining a point as strictly one-dimensional and avoid trying to figure out how that relates to three-dimensions altogether. Even if you try to say that a more valid two-dimensional relationship between a point as an area would be equal to a point squared as a unit of measurement, and likewise that a more valid in some sense unit of measurement of a point's volume would be a point cubed, none of the possible shapes that could represent a point as a three-dimensional limit simultaneously have a width, height, and depth of one point, an area of one point squared, and a volume of one point cubed. It is simply a mathematical and logical impossibility. If it has an area of one point squared, then its volume will be smaller than one point cubed, and if it has a volume of one point cubed, it will have an area that is bigger than one point squared. This at least calls into question the nature of one-dimensionally defined points in a three-dimensional context as absolute in the sense of the word. Even if the nature of points as strictly one-dimensionally, absolutely defined entities are somewhat concrete and constant, which it is to an extent, three-dimensional relationships with a one-dimensional point require some form of adaptation conceptually since three-dimensional space is concretely approachable as a continuum, which means that attempts to define its smallest parts are dependent on more than just one-dimensional relationships to some extent.

Third of all, if you were to utilize fractions of a point out of necessity since all possible three-dimensional applications would require or at least be subject to their potential use as a description, then there are an infinite number of possible ways to describe a limit that has a height, width, and depth of one point. This is because if space is a continuum in one light, then attempts to define its points that utilize infinitely divisible continuum logic provide infinite possible ways to define it. While none of the three-dimensional representations of a point work out idealistically in every way, three-dimensional representations of a point as a limit can be an infinitely diverse number of possible non-idealistic representations of a point. Different shapes could be used to describe different types of points as limits, and it may be that while the idea of a point is still, in one light, an absolute reference, there is room for infinite diversity within the context of how it relates to a three-dimensional continuum as a not absolute unit of nature. Since the philosophical definition of a point as strictly one-dimensional is logically absolutely defined and somewhat concrete on its own, and how that relates to three dimensions is logically somewhat definable, but how that relates to a three-dimensional continuum is possibly defined by infinite different possible manifestations logically, it is not illogical to expect nature to have to deal with the same paradox. In one light, this logically could entail that on the most fundamental level of how to define a point of space, or at least how they relate to three dimensions, there are literally infinite ways to do it for nature itself. There would be some somewhat constant aspects, like the concretely precise, absolute style, strictly one-dimensional definition of a point, and some room for diversity involving how that concrete idea is related to and translates into concretely continuum type of logic involved in two and three-dimensional contexts.

If the nature of points in an absolute, strictly one-dimensional sense is something that nature itself has to deal with, then there is still some room for some degree of consistency in its applications thereof. It is not untenable to think that, to some extent, nature would have to deal with one-dimensional points or that it is still somewhat concrete to refer to just one dimension of something in nature. This is because even if absolutely defined, one-dimensional points are, to an extent, an abstraction. The abstraction is concrete enough that we know exactly, with an infinite amount of precision even, what we are talking about when we refer to a strictly one-dimensional point. Since it is not to say that points are in every light only abstract and that it is theoretically impossible to expect some amount of correlation between the abstraction of one-dimensional points and three-dimensional reality, it is reasonable to expect some amount of correlation between the abstraction of one-dimensional points and concrete reality.

The fact that there are multiple ways of relating a one-dimensional point to a three-dimensional context could just be part of the nature of space, and it is not unreasonable to expect there to be multiple approaches to the same problem, even when it comes to the basics, like how to define units of space itself. This issue, in particular, could be interpreted as a sound enough theoretical reason to expect the unexpected to an extent, as we observe in the science of quantum mechanics. If nature has to deal with the notion of points somehow, and there are infinite different ways to manifest the nature of the relationship with the three-dimensional space of every point involved, that still has certain notions like points in common. We could expect to see the type of probability-based interpretations involved in the uncertainty principle. There would be enough consistency philosophically provided by the somewhat constant notions of points and instants to still expect to see trends in the probabilities, but not enough rigidity of the constants involved to expect to see complete predictability.

Extra Dimensions, Fractions of a Point, Fractals, and A Unified Theory

On the topic of a unified theory, the parallels between fractions of a point and the concept of extra dimensions could be important. It is easy to see how the notion of fractions of a point can seem like extra dimensions in a sense. In one light, a point is supposed to be, by definition, as small as possible and is as concrete as we can be about the smallest possible units of space. In another light, however, the continuum nature of space philosophically requires some compensation from point-based theory. The result is something that could be called extra dimensions of space, which everything could have in common. It is analogous to extra dimensions because the theoretical divisibility of a theoretical smallest unit could be seen in one light as extra-dimensional. In another light, however, they are not even extra dimensions, just logical compensation for the limitations of point-based logic in a continuum context. Since every type of continuum-based three-dimensional relationship with the concept of a point could be described with the use of fractions of a point somehow, it would be expected to find the notion of extra dimensions as fundamental to any attempts at a unified scientific theory that utilized points and continuum logic. These types of *extra* dimensions would be a fairly concrete interpretation of the possible meanings of the phrase extra dimensions. They could be expected to be a useful tool for any attempts to describe everything. One possible reconciliation of point-based logic and continuum reality of space-time could be Fractal space-time and a fractal matrix of fractal points. Because everything is entangled, every specific would affect the whole, and the whole would affect every specific. Fractal mathematics and quantum mechanical models could be combined as a structural mechanism for a unified theory and could possibly be implemented holographically in a self-similar, infinitely scalable system. A truly comprehensive unified theory should also probably factor in the unified field and universal background radiation, as well as consciousness, subjectivity, individuality, specificity, cosmometry, infinitesimals, and diversity. The mathematical equation Infinity multiplied by an infinitesimal equals 1 is an intriguing glimpse into philosophical reasoning for an infinitely dense, infinitely small, infinitely hot singularity like the Big Bang, and could be implemented in a universal String Theory Brane matrix of fractal quantum possibilities which serves as a mathematical ether, with fractions of a point representing fractaly encoded extra-dimensional strings that could function as an intelligently designed, adaptive, and evolving framework for nature with infinite possible manifestations and universal repercussions, possibly functioning as a fifth universal abstract mathematical dimension of sorts within which the other four-dimensional space-time continuum exists.